All the Women in the Bible:

The Women Around Jesus

Christine M. Carpenter

CMC Press, Portland, Oregon

To every girl or woman
who has had an encounter
with Jesus—
or ever hopes to.

Copyright © 1996 Christine M. Carpenter

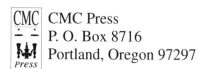 CMC Press
P. O. Box 8716
Portland, Oregon 97297

Scripture quotations from the New Revised Standard Version of the Bible are copyright © 1989 by the Division of Christian Education of the National Council of the Churches of Christ in the U.S.A. and are used by permission.

Library of Congress Catalogue Card Number: 96-86622

ISBN 1-887999-53-1 (Volume 1)
ISBN 1-887999-56-6 (6 Volume Set)

Contents

Chapter Three: Caught Adulteress

Chapter Four: Martha of Bethany

Chapter Five: Hemorrhaging Woman

Chapter Six: Canaanite/Syro-Phoenician Woman

Chapter Seven: Mary of Bethany

Chapter Eight: Mary Magdalene

Acknowledgments

I would like to acknowledge, for their *generosity* and *consideration,* the Division of Christian Education of the National Council of Churches of Christ in the U.S.A., because the Scripture quotations printed in this book are from the New Revised Standard Version of the Bible, copyright © 1989 by the Division of Christian Education of the National Council of Churches of Christ in the U.S.A., and are used by permission. All rights reserved. Their generosity and consideration of the needs of others, in assisting the reading of the scriptures, is to be commended. Therefore, it is with their permission that we are able to make the Holy Scriptures available in each chapter of this book.

I would like to acknowledge, for their *awareness* and *knowledge,* the women and men who are listed in the Selected References/Readings at the back of this book. Because they presented opportunities to rethink both the oldest and the newest interpretations and thoughts concerning the women in the Bible. Through them, once again, my confidence in the truth has been reconfirmed and my own work has been challenged. As a result of their input, this book is better.

I would like to acknowledge, for their *tactfulness* and *wisdom,* the women who have provided me with feedback that has challenged and enlightened me along this journey in and out of the lives of the women in the Bible. Because of these women today, my confidence in the truths presented in this book is surer, my writing more assertive, and my understanding clearer. In my garden of special women are so many beautiful flowers that I cannot mention each variety by name, but they know I am enriched by them and pray that they continue to bloom, sharing their beauty and fragrance with all.

I would like to acknowledge, for her *friendship* and *truthfulness,* Jeanette Soby, a better friend each year and an inspiring colleague who has let me learn from her, because she has often blazed the trail before me. She is always a light to my path and an encouragement to my life. She is God's instrument for good in my life. Words spoken by her have become my mottos: "There are NO shortages with God." "God is a God of endless opportunities." "God knows best, so I must be ready!" She is helium for my balloon! Again, this book is better because Jeanette has shared her time, energy, and ideas to make it so.

I would like to acknowledge, for his *love* and *willingness,* Kevin Shilts, my husband, because he has loved me regardless of, in spite of, and without reservation—demonstrating his willingness to do what and to go where God leads us. Kevin is the most special and giving person I have ever known. He is my role-model and mentor in developing my virtues. He has also shared in helping make this book what I wanted it to be.

I would like to acknowledge, for their *affection* and *generosity,* my children and grandchildren: Ron, Dana, David William, Teanna Virginia, Gary, Shannon, Tiffany Nichole, Krystal Leigh, Erica, Kelvin, Gizelle Elizabeth, and Alexander David, as my time and energies have gone into researching and writing this book. They are each my special joy on earth.

Finally, again, I would like to acknowledge that it is the Spirit of truth who has guided me into the *truth* I grow in, live by, and share. And I acknowledge God's faithfulness and blessing upon me and this book. If any praise is due, may it go to God, forever. If any corrections are due, may they come to me, personally, and as soon as possible.

Preface

The sentimental feelings we all have for those things we were educated to believe sacred, do not readily yield to pure reason. I distinctly remember the shudder that passed over me on seeing a mother take our family Bible to make a high seat for her child at table. It seemed such a desecration. I was tempted to protest against its use for such a purpose, and this, too, long after my reason had repudiated its divine authority.

Elizabeth Cady Stanton
The Woman's Bible

It is easy for me to relate to the concept of the sacredness of the Bible, as Elizabeth Cady Stanton recounted. So sacred was the Holy Bible in our family, that when a puppy, left alone in my grandfather's car, began teething on the Bible in the front seat, the puppy was immediately sentenced to the dog pound. Compromising the cover of the Sacred Book is difficult enough for many people to handle, but questioning the handed-down interpretation of its contents is even more reprehensible.

But question we must if we are to make sense of the Holy Scriptures, relating them to us, today. In fact, inheriting someone else's interpretation is irresponsible Christianity. Yet, where women in the Bible are concerned, most of us have probably encountered only a few women in the Bible at Sunday school, religious school, church, or synagogue. Perhaps as children or even as adults, the exposure was limited and focused more on a specific event rather than on the life of the particular woman. The interpretations of these encounters generally serve the purpose of the interpreter, rather than openly exploring what they can mean for us today.

Where the women in the Bible are concerned, generally we have seen only brief glimpses of them as supporting characters in stories focusing on men. The women around Jesus are no exception. Granted, Jesus is the main character in any story in which he appears, but he would have a limited starring role in the Bible without the Samaritan Woman at the Well or the Caught Adulteress or the Canaanite/Syro-Phoenician Woman or Martha of Bethany or the Hemorrhaging Woman or Mary of Bethany or Mary Magdalene. It is only when we see Jesus played off such as these that we see Jesus in his manifest compassion, wisdom, and power.

Yes, Jesus is the star, but it is my desire to share more fully the lives, limitations, strengths, and virtues of the women around Jesus in the Bible. My intention is that this book—focusing on biblical women—be stimulating, enlightening, and encouraging to those who encounter it. My prayer for you is that you may be blessed as you study these women around Jesus in the Bible. For all of us, may the encounters of these Bible women whet our thirst for our own encounters with Jesus.

As we consider and learn from the women around Jesus in the Bible, I acknowledge my *trust* in God, that the words of Jesus will be true for me as well as for you as we move to new dimensions of truth, daily. Gladly, I remind us all, that Jesus said that *"When the Spirit of truth comes, he will guide you into all the truth..."* (John 16:13). May you find this part of your life journey a blessing as you (re)discover that *"Jesus Christ is the same yesterday and today and forever"* (Hebrews 13:8).

Christine Carpenter

Introduction

Why This Book?

Unlike the Garden of Eden, the Bible is a source women can return to, and as with all great works of literature, it is a book that changes as we change. For curiosity we are thrown out of the Garden, and with curiosity we return.

Christina Buchmann and Celina Spiegel
Editors of *Out of the Garden*

Why I Wrote This Book

One reason I wrote this book was because each year I find more curiosity about the women in the Bible, from both women and men. While information about Bible women is available in the Bible, in a variety of commentaries, and in books from many different perspectives, usually the information is doled out in increments too small to satisfy the curious. So it should not be a surprise that again, I have been asked to research and write a more complete synopsis of the stories of the women around Jesus.

A second reason for writing this book is to remind us all of what Jesus did for those who asked. "Asking for help, rather than being a sign of weakness, is a sign of strength because it demonstrates humility," writes Dee Brestin in *We Are Sisters*. Continuing, she adds that it is "...the recognition that there are times in my life when I need help to carry an overburden. And if the need is genuine, rather than straining a friendship, asking for help cements it."

Many of the women around Jesus in this book asked for help. In all cases, the women in this book got what they needed from Jesus—sometimes without asking. In the process, each woman around Jesus went away from her encounter with Jesus well cemented in her relationship with him. She left him feeling that she was accepted, valued, and often elevated personally, spiritually, physically, mentally, and socially.

A third reason for writing this book is that today's woman needs to reconnect with the women around Jesus and identify with each woman as much as possible. Because as we hear each woman around Jesus speak to him or to herself, we can begin to hear ourselves ask Jesus for help with our overburden. As we see each woman around Jesus receive what she needs from God through Jesus, we can begin to see ourselves receiving our need met from God through Jesus.

Why Read This Book

- Do you want to know how the women around Jesus in the Bible interacted with him as well as you know how the men in the Bible interacted with Jesus? If you read this book you will begin to better know how the Bible women around Jesus behaved around him.

- Do you want to see and experience the women around Jesus in the Bible as real people to whom you can relate in your own life? If you read this book you will begin to better know the ways of success and failure through the life experiences of Bible women around Jesus.

- Do you want to expand your understanding of yourself and Jesus? If you read this book you will begin to better know who you are and who Jesus is—*Jesus Christ is the same yesterday and today and forever* (Hebrews 13:8).

What will be the benefits of reading this book?
- You will know more of what others believe about the women around Jesus in the Bible.
- You will know more of what you believe about the women around Jesus in the Bible.
- You will know more of what you believe about the role of a woman today.
- You will know more of what you believe about your role as a woman today.
- You will know more of what you believe about the role of Jesus today.

How to Use This Book

This book is designed for busy people! Each chapter has several smaller sections focusing on a particular topic related to that chapter's subject, so that the reader may use this book a section at a time. Most chapters contain the following:

Scripture: Chapter One is an overview and contains the listings of the women around Jesus, first by scripture references and then by brief summaries. Chapters Two through Eight focus on a particular woman around Jesus and contain scripture passages relating to her and her encounter with Jesus. In a group, each person may be invited to read aloud a section of scripture, a question with its possible choices, or to share an answer or thought. Committed groups may want to come prepared to discuss the material studied independently since the group last met.

Discussion Questions: Chapter One does not contain discussion questions, but suggests that the maps be used to find the locations of where the women around Jesus lived and encountered him. Chapters Two through Eight begin with discussion questions to ponder and answer.

Background Information: Each section of each chapter is intended to raise as many questions as it answers, in order to help you think through your own beliefs about the women around Jesus in the Bible. Also, questioning will help you sort out your own feelings and intentions toward the women in your life, and toward Jesus.

Reflection: Each chapter Reflection ties together the information presented in the chapter, giving commentary and practical application for today.

Summary & Focus Virtue: Each chapter focusing on a particular woman around Jesus has a summary of her story, a focus virtue she demonstrated, and how that focus virtue can be used today.

Virtues Reflection: Each chapter contains discussion questions relating to the focus virtue(s) demonstrated by that particular woman around Jesus. In groups, a time of sharing is appropriate at this point. One person may want to respond to all questions before going on to the next person, or everyone may be given an opportunity to respond to the current question before going on to the next question.

Action Scripture: Each chapter presents a scripture which is intended to inspire and motivate the reader in the focus areas encountered through the story of that particular woman around Jesus. It may be read and discussed first, or it may be read silently by all, or read aloud by the leader or designated person, or aloud in unison.

Grateful Prayer: At the conclusion of each chapter is a prayer which may be read silently by all, aloud by the leader or designated person, or aloud in unison.

In addition, interspersed throughout the book are maps, diagrams, and tables that are valuable resources for other chapters as well.

Chapter One

The Women Around Jesus Overview

Women today who seek to be around Jesus will find the same Jesus who is still including, teaching, feeding, healing, setting-free, restoring, defending, forgiving, and blessing women.

Christine M. Carpenter

Scripture References to Some of the Women Around Jesus

Woman	Matthew	Mark	Luke	John
Anointing Sinner			7:36-50	
Anointer at Simon the Leper's	26:1-2,6-13	14:3-9		
Canaanite/Syro-Phoenician Woman	15:21-28	7:24-30		
Caught Adulteress				8:3-11
Crippled Woman in Synagogue			13:10-13	
Galilean Women at the Cross	27:55	15:41	23:49, 55	
Hemorrhaging Woman	9:20-22	5:25-34	8:43-48	
Jairus' Wife & Daughter	9:18, 23-25	5:22, 24, 35-42	8:40-42, 49-55	
Joanna			8:1-3 24:1-11	
Martha of Bethany			10:38-42	11:1-45 12:1-2
Mary of Bethany			10:38-42	11:1-45 12:1-8

	Matthew	Mark	Luke	John
Mary, Clopas' wife				19:25
Mary Magdalene	27:56, 61 28:1-11	15:40, 47 16:1, 9	8:2-3 24:1-12	19:25 20:1-2, 11-18
Mary, Mother of James and Joseph	27:56, 61 28:1-11	15:40, 47 16:1	24:10	
Mary of Nazareth	12:46-50	3:31-35	8:19-21	2:1-11 19:25-27
Mary of Nazareth's Sister				19:25
Peter's Mother-in-law	8:14-15	1:30-31	4:38-39	
Salome		15:40 16:1		
Samaritan Woman at the Well				4:5-43
Susanna			8:1-3	
Widow Giving Her Offering		12:42-43	12:2-3	
Widow of Nain			7:11-15	
Women Supporters of Jesus' Ministry	27:55		8:1-3; 23:49; 24:10	
Zebedee's Wife	20:20-23 27:56			

Summaries of the Women Around Jesus

ANOINTING SINNER
Luke 7:36-50

Early in Jesus' ministry she went to the house of Simon the Pharisee where Jesus was a dinner guest. This sinner woman of the city intruded, and began weeping, enough so that she bathed the feet of Jesus with her tears and dried them with her hair—repeatedly kissing his feet and anointed them with the ointment she brought with her. When Jesus sensed the disapproval of her actions by his host he defended her by telling the Pharisee a parable about love and forgiveness. Then Jesus told the anointing sinner that her faith had saved her and that she should go in peace.

ANOINTER AT SIMON THE LEPER'S
Matthew 26:1-2, 6-13; Mark 14:3-9

This unnamed woman at Simon the leper's house, in Bethany, anointed the head of Jesus. It was two days before Jesus would eat his last Passover before his crucifixion. She remains a mystery woman, but this we know, she anointed the head of Jesus—a ceremonial act symbolizing God's power upon the one anointed to begin an official office. Israel anointed each of its succeeding kings in such a way to signify that he was "God's anointed one—the Messiah" who would deliver them and establish the presence of God on earth. Jesus said that she had done a good service for him and it would be told in remembrance of her wherever the Good News was told. Some scholars believe that this woman's anointing for the Kingship of the Christ was what made the good news possible as Jesus went from the cross into Abraham's Bosom and set the captives free.

BRIDE OF CANA OF GALILEE
John 2:1-11

Through the encouragement of Mary of Nazareth, the mother of Jesus, this bride's wedding celebration, instead of running out of wine, was supplied with the best of wine when Jesus performed his first public miracle.

CANAANITE/SYRO-PHOENICIAN WOMAN
Matthew 15:21-28; Mark 7:24-30

First she was ignored by Jesus when she called after him for help. Then the disciples of Jesus asked him to send her away. But this woman persisted in calling out for the help of Jesus, because she had a daughter who needed to be healed. Her shouts of faith got her an audience with Jesus, despite the disciples' aggravation toward her and their protection of Jesus. She humbly knelt before Jesus who continued to speak with her, eventually granting her request—because of her great faith.

CAUGHT ADULTERESS
John 8:3-11

Hebrew law required both the man and woman caught in adultery to be put to death. However, in this case, only this woman was set before Jesus and the crowd as an object lesson of sin. She was brought for judgement and humiliation, her partner never being mentioned. Probably half-naked and disheveled, required by the scribes and Pharisees to stand facing Jesus, her accusers departed one by one beginning with the elders—without condemning her—as Jesus silently wrote on the ground, waiting for the person without sin to cast the first stone. Then Jesus told her that he did not condemn her either—nor should she sin in this way again.

CRIPPLED WOMAN IN SYNAGOGUE
Luke 13:10-13

For eighteen years this woman had been crippled, yet her bent-over body was present in the synagogue on the sabbath when Jesus entered with his disciples to teach that day. She was unable to straighten herself and stand normally. When Jesus saw her he called her to him, and she obeyed. Then Jesus, laying his hands on her, verbally loosed her from her condition and immediately she stood tall and began glorifying God. When rebuked by the ruler of the synagogue, Jesus defended this woman's right to be free from her affliction at the first opportunity—sabbath or not.

DAUGHTERS OF JERUSALEM
Luke 23:27-31

These women were bemoaning Jesus' carrying the cross to his own death. As they expressed their sorrow for him he paused to express his sorrow for them in the desolate times to come—referring to the fall of Jerusalem in 70 A.D.

GALILEAN WOMEN AT THE CROSS
Matthew 27:55; Mark 15:41; Luke 23:49, 55

These women must have been too numerous to name individually, however, some of their foremost leaders received honorable mention—one as the wife of an important official for Herod Antipas, another as the wife of a prosperous fisherman, and another being the mother of prominent men in Jesus' circle of followers, as well as some women named as special observers of the crucifixion, the burial, and the resurrection of Jesus—and bearers of its announcement.

HEMORRHAGING WOMAN
Matthew 9:20-22; Mark 5:25-34; Luke 8:43-48

After twelve years of blood draining weakness, endless laundering, and financial poverty from extensive doctors visits and treatments, the bleeding of the Hemorrhaging Woman continued unabated. In addition, the Jewish law decreed her as unclean, cursed, and contagious. Under the law she was not allowed to touch anyone or anything anyone would touch. But she touched the hem of the garment of Jesus. Jesus stopped and confronted the crowd. She came forward and told him all. He commended her faith and sent her away healed and in peace, calling her "daughter".

JAIRUS' WIFE
Matthew 9:18, 23-25; Mark 5:22, 24, 35-42; Luke 8:40-42, 49-55

She was the wife of an official in charge of the services and care of the synagogue. When her husband returned home with Jesus, Jairus' wife had already begun to mourn the death of their twelve-year-old daughter. In the midst of the wailing mourners, Jesus sent away everyone and entered the girl's death chamber with only her mother and father, and Jesus' disciples, Peter, James, and John. Jesus took her hand and told the girl to rise and she stood up. Then Jesus told them to give the girl something to eat.

JAIRUS' DAUGHTER

Matthew 9:18, 23-25; Mark 5:22, 24, 35-42; Luke 8:40-42, 49-55

She was the twelve-year-old daughter of an important synagogue official. When she became ill her father went to find Jesus to ask him to come and heal her. Jesus was delayed and she died. Jesus told her father, Jairus, to believe and they went to the girl. Mourning had begun by the time they arrived, but Jesus sent away everyone and entered the girl's death chamber with only her mother and father, and Jesus' disciples, Peter, James, and John. Jesus took the girl's hand and told the her to rise and she stood up. Then the Great Physician prescribed food to be given to the girl.

JOANNA

Luke 8:1-3; 24:1-11

Joanna was the wife of Chuza, the steward of Herod Antipas. Jesus healed or delivered her from an unmentioned condition and she became his follower and supporter: giving her time, energies, and financial means to the work of the Lord. She was one of the women who went early to the tomb of Jesus and among the first to learn of the resurrection—reporting it in person with the others to the disciples of Jesus, but they did not believe her.

MARTHA

Luke 10:38-42; John 11:1-45; 12:1-2

Martha of Bethany invited Jesus into her home and entertained Jesus and his disciples on many occasions. Jesus became her spiritual teacher, friend, and Messiah. When Martha's brother Lazarus became very ill, Martha and her sister sent for Jesus. Jesus delayed and Lazarus died. When Martha confronted Jesus as Messiah—Jesus raised Lazarus from the dead.

MARY OF BETHANY

Luke 10:38-42; John 11:1-45; 12:1-8

Mary of Bethany was sister to Martha, and Lazarus whom Jesus raised from the dead. Mary of Bethany sat at the feet of Jesus, listening to him as her sister Martha prepared to serve Jesus and the other guests. When Mary of Bethany was criticized by Martha for not helping, Jesus defended Mary of Bethany's desire to be present in spiritual matters. Later, the week before the crucifixion of Jesus, Mary of Bethany anointed the feet of Jesus with costly perfume, and wiped them with her hair. When Judas criticized Mary of Bethany for the financial waste—approximately one year's wages for a laborer—Jesus defended Mary and proclaimed that her deed was preparation for his burial.

MARY, CLOPAS' WIFE

John 19:25

This woman was one of the women present at the crucifixion of Jesus. She may have been the same woman who is identified as Mary, the mother of James, Joseph/Joses, and Salome. A poor case has been made for this woman being the sister of Mary, the mother of Jesus. It has been too difficult for most skeptics to rationalize two sisters having the same name—Mary. Whoever she was related to, on the day of the crucifixion she stood in distinguished company with the Mary of Nazareth—mother of Jesus, the sister of Mary of Nazareth, and Mary Magdalene.

MARY MAGDALENE

Matthew 27:56, 61; 28:1-11; Mark 15:40, 47; 16:1, 9; Luke 8:2-3; 24:1-12; John 19:25; 20:1-2, 11-18

Mary Magdalene was a devout follower, supporter, and friend of Jesus. She traveled with him as he taught and healed—herself being healed by him. She stayed with him as he hung on the cross and went with him to his tomb. She prepared burial spices, with other women, and went with them to his tomb—unexpectedly seeing Jesus in his glorified resurrected body—before he ascended to his Father in Heaven. Later, Jesus returned and showed himself to the disciples and scolded them for not believing Mary Magdalene who had carried Jesus' message to them.

MARY, MOTHER OF JAMES AND JOSEPH

Matthew 27:56, 61; 28:1-11; Mark 15:40, 47; 16:1; Luke 24:10

Mary was one of the women present at the crucifixion of Jesus. She watched as Jesus was put into the tomb of Joseph of Arimathea. With other women, she helped prepare burial spices and returned with the other women to anoint the body of Jesus. She was among those women who first saw the empty tomb and heard the news of the resurrection of Jesus. She may have been the same woman identified as the wife of Clopas.

MARY OF NAZARETH

Matthew 12:46-50; Mark 3:31-35; Luke 8:19-21; John 19:25-27

Twice the angel Gabriel told the virgin Mary she was favored by God to bare the Messiah. When she gave birth in a stable, among the animals, the angels sent shepherds to greet the Messiah of Mary. Wise men brought him gifts. Mary's confirmations of Jesus and his mission continued in just weeks after his birth when they went to the temple to make the required sacrifice after childbirth. In the Temple, Anna and Simeon both openly declared her babe the long awaited Messiah! As a mother she watched her firstborn grow in grace and favor with God. After the crucifixion, the LORD provided for Mary by including her in the company of those who loved her son Jesus. She accepted her extended family and was in their midst on the day of Pentecost.

MARY OF NAZARETH'S SISTER

John 19:25

This woman was the sister of Mary, the mother of Jesus. She stood close to the cross with Mary through the crucifixion of Jesus. There is uncertainty as to exactly who was the sister of Mary of Nazareth. Some think she was Mary, Clopas' wife. Others doubt that sisters would both go by the name of Mary. The confusion and uncertainty about the name of Mary's sister is due to the ambiguous wording of John 19:25.

PETER'S MOTHER-IN-LAW

Matthew 8:14-15; Mark 1:30-31; Luke 4:38-39

This woman was in bed with a high fever at dinner-time, but Jesus stood over her and healed her. She felt well enough to immediately get up and begin serving them all.

PILATE'S WIFE

Matthew 27:19

To no avail, this Jewish woman sent a note to her husband during the trial of Jesus, stating that she had been warned in a dream that Jesus was a just man and not to be a party to bring harm to him.

SALOME

Matthew 20:20-23; 27:56; Mark 15:40; 16:1

Believed to be the wife of Zebedee, a prosperous fisherman. If so, she was also the mother of James and John, and on at least one occasion she would have asked Jesus for special favors for her sons in Jesus' kingdom. Without dispute, she became a disciple of Jesus and was one of the women present at his crucifixion and one of the women who helped prepare spices for the proper burial of Jesus' entombed body.

SAMARITAN WOMAN AT THE WELL

John 4:5-43

This woman, who had been wife to five husbands and was not married to the man she lived with then, came to draw water from Jacob's Well when Jesus asked her for a drink. Their repartee continued several rounds as Jesus answered her questions, understood and accepted her, then revealed himself as the Messiah. She left her water pot and went to get the townspeople to come and meet the Messiah. They listened, believed, and followed her back to the well where they asked Jesus to stay with them; he stayed there two days. As a result, many believed in Jesus.

SISTERS OF JESUS
Matthew 13:56; Mark 6:3

Along with their mother and brothers, the sisters of Jesus came to speak with Jesus while he was teaching. They claimed no special place in the ministry of Jesus, nor did he give them special treatment.

SUSANNA
Luke 8:1-3

This woman, who had been cured of unknown ailments by Jesus, became his follower. Going from city to city, she supported Jesus with her time, energies, and finances. She may have been one of the women identified in the gospels as being among the "other women" or "certain women" who followed Jesus and were at the crucifixion.

WIDOW GIVING HER OFFERING
Mark 12:42-43; Luke 12:2-3

This widow caught the attention of Jesus as he was teaching against the hypocrisy of the scribes, noting their desire for recognition, seeking of the best positions, stealing from the helpless, and acting with pretense about their religiosity. Somehow Jesus knew that this woman was a widow and all she had left was the equivalent of less than a penny. As she deposited her last two mites into the offering, Jesus commended her because she gave all she had to God.

WIDOW OF NAIN
Luke 7:11-15

This woman was a resident of the town of Nain in the region of Galilee. Her husband was already dead when her only son died. When Jesus saw her, he had compassion on her. As the son's funeral processed, he interrupted the ceremony by first telling this bereaved woman not to weep, then he touched the casket and he told her son to rise. The son sat up and spoke; Jesus presented the young man to his mother.

WOMAN WHO BLESSED JESUS' MOTHER
Luke 11:27-28

Jesus had just cast out a mute demon and when it was gone the mute spoke. But the crowd was divided—some thinking Jesus had power over the demon because Jesus had a connection with Satan. Jesus spoke up and refuted that idea, acknowledging his power from God. As he spoke, this unnamed woman in the crowd raised her voice, saying to Jesus, "Blessed is the womb that bore you and the breasts that nursed you!" Could she have been expressing her gratitude for the miracle of voice coming from the mute person who may have been a loved one of hers?

WOMEN AT THE FEEDING OF 4,000 & 5,000
Matt. 15:32-38; Mark 8:1-9 & Matt. 14:15-21; Mark 6:35-44; Luke 9:11-17; John 6:5-14

After lengthy teaching sessions, Jesus performed miracles for his hearers, increasing the quantity of food available so that everyone could eat their fill—including women and children, in addition to the men counted in the first group of 5,000 and the second group of 4,000.

WOMEN SUPPORTERS OF JESUS' MINISTRY
Matthew 27:55; Mark 15:40; Luke 8:1-3; 23:49; 24:10

Among these unnamed women were those who had been cured of various ailments. Some of the women provided for Jesus financially as well as being present at his crucifixion, burial, and resurrection.

ZEBEDEE'S WIFE—SEE SALOME

By combining Mark 16:1 and Matthew 27:56, Zebedee's wife is believed to be Salome. In addition, some scholars use John 19:25 as evidence that she is also the sister of Mary of Nazareth, making her the aunt of Jesus, and her sons James and John cousins of Jesus.

Overview of the Ministry of Jesus

The ministry of Jesus touched the lives of men, women, and children. Who, what, where, when, why, and how will be briefly summarized in this section. More information on Jesus' encounters, with women in particular, are included in the table, *Summaries of The Women Around Jesus,* at the beginning of this chapter. In succeeding chapters of this book—as well as in this author's previous book, *All the Women in the Bible: Sisters & Sisterhood*—are more detailed encounters between Jesus and specific women in the New Testament.

Who and What?

Jesus went about doing good and healing all who were oppressed, as the scriptures clearly demonstrate. The individuals and groups with whom he interacted were from a variety of demographics. Most people identified in the Gospels can easily be classified into one or more categories of society. Some examples include: gender, age, health or fitness, ethnicity or race, national origin, family heritage, social status, occupation or profession, economic status or power, family or marital status, training or education, religion or politics, and personality or temperament.

Specifically, Jesus found himself or put himself around both male and female genders. For instance, his traveling ministry was comprised of both men and women. In addition, he ministered in a variety of ways to both sexes, by teaching, warning, and healing.

Also, folks of all ages were found in the company of Jesus. One such age based situation involved the blessing of children. On another occasion, a specific child, a girl twelve-years-old, was raised from the dead by Jesus. Another age based encounter included a young man who had many possessions and went away from Jesus saddened because he could not give them away and follow the Christ.

Especially the unhealthy or unfit came to Jesus. They came as the blind, the deaf, and the mute. They came lame, withered, and bent-over. They came fevered, leperous, and hemorrhaging. They came epileptic, crippled, and paralyzed. They came possessed, oppressed, and tormented. All went away cured, many receiving blessings and the forgiveness of their sins.

Jesus was sent to the Jews first, but he also ministered to people of other ethnicities or races. He not only spoke to a Syro-Phoenician woman, but also spoke the Word that delivered her daughter. At another time and place he began talking with a Samaritan woman and ended by residing with and teaching for two days in her town—filled with Samaritan women and men. At another time, a Roman centurion came to Jesus asking for the healing of his paralyzed servant, whom Jesus healed just as the centurion asked. Also demonstrating that Jesus became involved with people who were not "Jerusalem Jews" was the fact that Jesus' disciple Simon was called the Canaanite.

While family heritage was highly rated in Jesus' day, he ministered to people no matter what their family heritage. On at least one occasion he reduced everyone's family heritage to one common family— the family of God. To paraphrase, he said that his mother, his father, his brothers, and his sisters were those who did the will of God, being children of God. In addition, he said that everyone should let go of their family in order to pursue the things of God.

Varied social status was the norm among persons with whom Jesus came into contact. Some examples include the rich young ruler, a crippled beggar, and a homemaker. Even the religious sects considered distinctions of social status between themselves and others of another sect. But Jesus entertained questions and accepted hospitality from everyone, equally: from nobleman, to business owner, to servant, to beggar.

The people who crossed the path of Jesus' ministry came from a variety of occupations or professions. Peter, James, and John were fishermen, Matthew and Zaccheus were a tax collectors, and most of the women were homemakers. Jesus had many encounters with scribes, priests, and eventually with the rulers of Judea and Galilee. Laborers, merchants, and farmers were prevalent, as indicated by parables told by Jesus. Everyone was welcomed into the presence of Jesus.

The economic status or power of those coming into contact with Jesus was diverse. At the low end of the scale were widows, lepers, and beggars. In the middle range of economic status or power were people like the master who sought the help of Jesus for his servant and Zebedee who had hired servants for his fishing boat fleet. At the high end of the scale were people like Annas and Caiaphas of the high priesthood or Pilate and Herod who held the life of Jesus in their hands.

Family or marital status varied widely among those who encountered Jesus. With the status of widow usually came poverty because the woman no longer had a husband to provide for her, unless sons or male relatives were willing to support her. On one occasion Jesus showed compassion for a widow, in Nain, who's only son had died, and returned him alive to his mother. Another time Jesus ministered to a family by going with Jairus and his wife into the room of their dead daughter and raising her to life again. Also,

Jesus raised from the dead Lazarus, the brother of Martha and Mary of Bethany—all three were single adults. In addition, the mother-in-law of Peter was raised up from her bed by Jesus and was then able to serve all who were present at the time of her healing. Finally, the children were important enough to Jesus so that he defended them and their spiritual rights, ultimately taking them to himself and giving them a blessing. In short, children, virgins, single, married, divorced, and widowed individuals were touched by Jesus and his ministry in some way, though teaching, healing, or blessing.

Jesus interacted with individuals from distinct differences in levels of training or education. The most obvious discrepancy in training or education would have been between children and scribes. Scribes formally studied all of their life and would not be fully ordained as a scribe until about age 40. Boys usually had formal schooling in the synagogue from five to ten years of age—for a half-day, six days a week. During those years he was also learning a trade or studying to become a scholarly scribe. Generally, girls and women received no formal training or education, which is why the invitation of Jesus for women to learn from him—Mary of Bethany first at his feet and then Martha—was revolutionary and attracted a group of women who travelled with Jesus.

The religion or politics of those talking with Jesus was extremely diverse. The Herodians supported Graeco-Roman policies and Hellenization of culture, accepting foreign rule and the status quo. The Herodians and Pharisees tried to trap Jesus by getting him to deny responsibility for paying Roman taxes.

The largest Jewish sect was Pharisees comprised of mostly middle class merchants and tradesmen.

Pharisees were monotheistic, strict sabbath observers of tithing and purification rituals. Pharisees believed in bodily resurrection of life after death, and the reality of demons and angels.

Another sect was Sadducees, only accepting the written Torah as the literal interpretation of the Law. Sadducees denied life after death, divine providence, demons and angels. The Sadducees tried to trap Jesus by asking him who's wife a woman would be in the resurrection, having had several brothers as husbands under Levirite marriage law.

One of many other sects was Zealots, believing that religion and politics were inseparable. Zealots opposed Roman rule, refusing to pay taxes, and engaging in terrorism against Rome. Judas Iscairot and Simon the Canaanite were Zealots before joining up with Jesus.

The strict ascetic Essenes rounded out the list of the five most prominent Jewish sects. Holding all things in common, these celibate pacifist Essenes believed in simplicity, the immortality of the soul but not the body. They held Hebrew scripture and other literature as authoritative. Rejecting Temple worship and offerings they lived apart from the community. This scholarly sect is credited with the preservation of the Dead Sea Scrolls. There is no scriptural record of Essenes approaching Jesus. However, some scholars believe that the cousin and baptizer of Jesus, John the Baptist, was part of the Essene community or influenced by Essenes.

The personalities or temperaments of individuals within the ministry of Jesus and of those being ministered to by Jesus varied greatly. Examples of assertiveness include Peter who cut off the ear of the high priest's servant in the Garden of Gethsemane, two blind men who shouted for Jesus to have mercy on them, a father who shouted for Jesus to look at his only son who was epileptic, and a woman who shouted to Jesus a blessing upon his mother. Not as assertive was the woman with a hemorrhage who was down at hem level when she touched the garment of Jesus. Others who knelt before Jesus include a leper who wanted to be made clean, the leader of a synagogue seeking healing for his daughter, and Mary of Bethany when she was mourning for her dead brother, Lazarus. Before that Mary of Bethany knelt at the feet of Jesus to learn about the scriptures. Many learners, both open- and closed-minded, came to hear the teaching of Jesus. Some people who heard Jesus were resisting sceptics while others were eager believers. Now as then, Jesus embraces all who will come to him.

Where and When

The chronology of events in the Gospels is far less certain than the locations described. However, a consensus has been reached for the location and timing of many of the encounters during the ministry of Jesus. Some descriptions include not only the main characters and interaction, but also the immediate physical surroundings, such as when Jesus taught from a boat anchored just offshore, or when he stood to read the scroll of Isaiah in a synagogue, or when he sat at the table to take a meal in the house of Simon the Pharisee.

In a wider picture the scriptures sometimes describe the general area. Some examples include a field where the disciples of Jesus picked grain on the sabbath, or a description of the road from the Mount of Olives to Jerusalem on what we call Palm Sunday, or the garden where, after his resurrection, Jesus first spoke to Mary Magdalene.

An even broader picture is seen when the scriptures identify a particular town or region, such as the time Jesus sent away the crowds and got into a boat set out for the region of Magadan, or when he returned from the region of Tyre and went by way of Sidon towards the Sea of Galilee, in the region of the Decapolis.

Some of the encounters between Jesus and women specifically identified in the scriptures, are in the following alphabetical list of places. The map of *Palestine During the Ministry of Jesus,* in this chapter, may be helpful in locating the general area of some of the encounters with Jesus. For locating some of the events listed for Jerusalem and its surrounding area, consult the *Jerusalem Area in the Time of Jesus* map found in Chapter 8, Mary Magdalene. [Note: Only one scripture reference is given for each event, but often the same account is given in other Gospels.]

Bethlehem, where Mary of Nazareth gave birth to Jesus (Luke 2:1-21).

Bethsaida, where Jesus fed women and children in addition to the 5,000 men after he spoke to them about the Kingdom of God and healed all who needed to be cured (Luke 9:10-17).

Bethany, at Martha's house, where she served hospitality to Jesus and his disciples, often, and Mary of Bethany sat at the feet of Jesus, learning spiritual lessons and concepts (Luke 10:38-42).

Bethany, at Lazarus' tomb, where Jesus resurrected the brother of Mary of Bethany and Martha, after Martha had a dialogue with Jesus in which

19

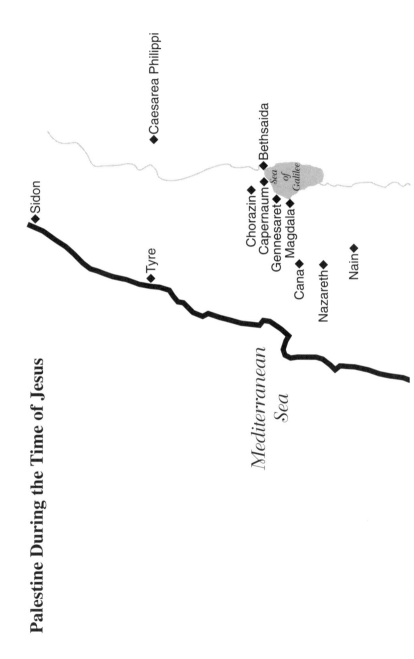

Palestine During the Time of Jesus

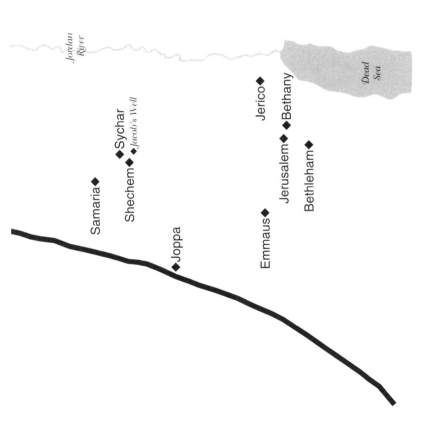

she declared Jesus Messiah (John 11:1-45).

Bethany, at Lazarus' house, where Martha served Jesus and Mary of Bethany anointed the feet of Jesus six days before the Passover (Luke 12:1-8).

Bethany, at Simon the Leper's house, where an un-named woman anointed the head of Jesus two days before the Passover (Matthew 26:1-2, 6-13).

Bethphage at the Mount of Olives, where Jesus began his triumphal entry into Jerusalem and was joined along the way with shouts from the crowd that included women who said, "Hosanna to the Son of David! Blessed is the one who comes in the name of the Lord! Hosanna in the highest heaven!" (Matthew 21:1-11).

Caesarea Philippi, where tradition places the home-town of the Hemorrhaging Woman (see page 149).

Calvary/Golgotha/Place of the Skull, where women observed the crucifixion of Jesus, including Mary Magdalene, and Mary the mother of James and Joseph, and the mother of the sons of Zebedee (Matthew 27:55-56).

Cana, where at the request of his mother, Jesus turned water into wine at a wedding feast (John 2:1-11).

Caiaphas' house, where servant girls questioned Peter's association with Jesus and Peter denied knowing Jesus (Matthew 26:69-75).

Capernaum, a city in Galilee, where Jesus healed

Peter's mother-in-law (Luke 4:31-39).

District of Tyre and Sidon, where a Canaanite/Syro-Phoenician woman asked Jesus for help for her demon tormented daughter and the demon left (Matthew 15:21-28).

Garden of Gethsemane, where Jesus was arrested. Tradition says that Martha and Mary of Bethany may have been present along with Mary Magdalene and the other female disciples of Jesus (Matthew 26:47-56).

Jerusalem, at the Praetorium, where Pilate pronounced judgment on Jesus in spite of a warning from his wife (Matthew 27:19-26).

Jerusalem, in the streets, where women bemoaned Jesus carrying his cross to Golgotha (Luke 23:27-31).

Jerusalem, in the Temple, where Jesus forgave the Caught Adulteress; commended the offering of the destitute widow (John 8:3-11; Mark 12:42-43).

Magdala, where the Mary for whom Jesus cast out seven demons was from (Mark 16:9).

Nazareth, where Jesus' pre-ministry home was with his Mother Mary, and his sisters and brothers (Luke 2:39)

Nain, where without being requested to, Jesus raised from the dead the widow's only son (Luke 7:11-15).

Sychar, where Jesus talked with a Samaritan woman, revealing to her that he was Messiah (John 4:5-43).

Tomb of Joseph of Arimathea, where Mary Magdalene and the "other" Mary, as she is called in scripture, sat and watched as Jesus was buried by Joseph and Nicodemus; returned early the morning after the sabbath with spices to properly treat the body of Jesus; an angel appeared to them announcing the resurrection of Jesus; Jesus spoke to the women, giving them a message to deliver to the disciples (Matthew 27:57-61; Matthew 28:1-10)

How and Why

Both named and unnamed women in the New Testament Gospels are included in the Bible for a reason. How and why they are mentioned specifically in detail or vaguely in the shadows of others is not always easy to understand. Many scholars and laypersons have endeavoured to flush out, liven up, or tone down particular Bible women. Sometimes conjecture is used to fill in missing gaps. At other times pure fantasy is employed to get the desired result. However, in almost all cases, their sincere desire and effort to make these women even more real to us is to be applauded. On the other hand, making more or less of a Bible woman can be both deceiving and disappointing.

Therefore, the content of this book will attempt to encourage the reader to ponder Bible women in full light of what *is* and *is not* said about them in the scriptures. In addition, a sincere, unbiased effort will be made to suggest plausible explanations, and in some instances alternate explanations, for the thoughts, feelings, motivations, and actions of the women around Jesus.

As we explore the thoughts, feelings, motivations, and actions of these women we will find out more clues as to why they were mentioned in the Bible. One of the reasons they may have been mentioned could be for their demonstration of virtues. Even the most obscure woman uses one or more virtues.

Seeing Bible women in light of their virtues does more than enhance the reputation of a particular Bible woman. The demonstration of virtues by Bible women become positive role models for all individuals, and for women in particular. Some examples of virtues found in the following chapters of this book include the Samaritan Woman at the Well who demonstrated *Willingness*, the Caught Adulteress who demonstrated *Forgiveness*, Martha of Bethany who demonstrated *Friendliness*, the Hemorrhaging Woman who demonstrated *Gentleness*, the Canaanite/Syro-Phoenician Woman who demonstrated *Humility,* Mary of Bethany who demonstrated *Reverence*, and Mary Magdalene who demonstrated *Steadfastness*. Other examples of virtues demonstrated by specific women in the Bible are included in *All the Women in the Bible: Sisters & Sisterhood* and in the *Virtues Spiritual Growth Guide,* as well as being the focus of Bible Women Surprise Cards (All available through CMC Press).

Each chapter of this book contains a Virtues Reflection to consider and discuss. The "Focus Virtues" page in this chapter lists fifty-two Christian virtues. The multifaceted women who are the focus of Chapters Two through Eight all demonstrate many of these virtues at different times—and so do we!

Reflection

A person's self-concept is an important part of thinking and feeling that she or he is included in a group, such as Christians, or a concept, such as eternal life. When someone does not identify with a person or event it becomes difficult to create a relationship between them. Similarly, when women are expected to bridge the gap between who they are in this physical world and what they want to become in the spiritual world, women find it easier to make the journey across the sometimes treacherous waters of religion if sufficient landmarks guide them along the way.

Words used to describe women are female landmarks. Women who find female landmarks in the Bible often progress on their spiritual journey more quickly and with less frustration. Such helpful landmarks include the accounts of events about women and words identified with the female gender. Unfortunately, the stories of women as recorded in the Gospels of the New Testament in the Bible are too few in number.

Even the Gospel's references to females, according to the New Revised Standard Versions (NRSV) of the Bible, macBible 3.0, is far less than the references to males. For example, the word "woman" appears in a total of 57 verses in Matthew, Mark, Luke, and John. In the same Gospels, the word "man" appears 270 times. Also showing a marked discrepancy in the female term used in the Gospels are the words "mother" being mentioned in 68 verses while "father" is mentioned in 278 verses. But the greatest discrepancy is between the appearance of the word "daughter" and "son". The female is in 23 verses and the male in 315 verses.

In some other female and male comparisons the genders appear to be more evenly balanced. (For more details see the table entitled *Occurrences and Verses Referring to Female Identity in the Gospels* in this Reflection section.) One instance of a more even balance is between the words "girl" and "boy" which appear in 8 and 9 verses, respectively. In some instances, when you are reviewing the table, you may even notice that the female references out number the male references for the same type of comparison.

One example of the female out numbering the male is found in the comparison of the words "wife" and "husband". The word "wife" appears in 33 verses and "husband" appears in 9 verses, only. However, when a wife is mentioned in these verses it is generally to link her to her husband. These numbers are another reminder that women in the time of Jesus were considered as property and identified in terms of their male relationships. On the other hand, husbands generally stand alone as Bible characters and are rarely referred to in terms of their relationships to their wives or other females.

As we look at the few women mentioned by Matthew, Mark, Luke, and John, we are grateful for their inclusion—even when they remain unnamed. We can conjecture that one reason for the scarcity of women in the Gospels is that these writers were still in transition from the traditional concept of women as inferior to men, a distraction from the spiritual goals of males, and nonparticipants in religious matters (1Corinthians 14:34). Jesus turned up-side-down the idea of women as property that were to be used only to serve and to propagate.

Too often, even when their stories are included in the scriptures, Bible women have been silent. We

Occurrences and Verses Referring to Female Identity in the Gospels*

daughter = 23 (son = 315)

Matt. 9:18	Matt. 9:22	Matt. 10:35	Matt. 10:37	Matt. 14:6
Matt. 15:22	Matt. 15:28	Matt. 21:5	Mark 5:23	Mark 5:34
Mark 5:35	Mark 6:22	Mark 7:25	Mark 7:26	Mark 7:29
Luke 2:36	Luke 8:42	Luke 8:48	Luke 8:49	Luke 12:53
Luke 13:16	John 12:15			

daughters = 1 (sons = 12)

Luke 23:28

daughter-in-law = 2 (son-in-law = 0)

Matt. 10:35 Luke 12:53

daughters-in-law = 0 (sons-in-law = 0)

female = 2 (male = 3)

Matt. 19:4   Mark 10:6

females = 0 (males = 0)

girl = 8 (boy = 9)

Matt. 9:24	Matt. 9:25	Matt. 14:11	Mark 5:41	Mark 5:42
Mark 6:22	Mark 6:28			

girls = 0 (boys = 0)

mother = 68 (father = 278)

Matt. 1:18	Matt. 2:11	Matt. 2:13	Matt. 2:14	Matt. 2:20
Matt. 2:21	Matt. 10:35	Matt. 10:37	Matt. 12:46	Matt. 12:47
Matt. 12:48	Matt. 12:49	Matt. 12:50	Matt. 13:55	Matt. 14:8
Matt. 14:11	Matt. 15:4	Matt. 15:5	Matt. 19:5	Matt. 19:19
Matt. 19:29	Matt. 20:20	Matt. 27:56	Mark 3:31	Mark 3:32
Mark 3:33	Mark 3:34	Mark 3:35	Mark 5:40	Mark 6:24
Mark 6:28	Mark 7:10	Mark 7:11	Mark 7:12	Mark 10:7
Mark 10:19	Mark 10:29	Mark 15:40	Mark 15:47	Mark 16:1
Luke 1:43	Luke 1:60	Luke 2:33	Luke 2:34	Luke 2:48
Luke 2:51	Luke 7:15	Luke 8:19	Luke 8:20	Luke 8:21
Luke 8:51	Luke 12:53	Luke 14:26	Luke 18:20	Luke 24:10
John 2:1	John 2:3	John 2:5	John 2:12	John 6:42
John 19:25	John 19:26	John 19:27		

mothers = 4 (father's = 15)

Mark 10:30 Luke 7:12   John 3:4   John 19:25

mother-in-law = 5 (father in law = 1)

Matt. 8:14   Matt. 10:35 Mark 1:30   Luke 4:38   Luke 12:53

---

mothers-in-law = 0 (fathers-in-law = 0)

sister = 14 (brother = 43)

Matt. 5:22	Matt. 5:23	Matt. 5:24	Matt. 12:50	Matt. 18:35
Mark 3:35	Luke 10:39	Luke 10:40	John 11:1	John 11:5
John 11:28	John 11:39	John 19:25		

sisters = 9 (brothers = 36; brother's = 2)

Matt. 5:47	Matt. 13:56	Matt. 19:29	Mark 3:32	Mark 6:3
Mark 10:29	Mark 10:30	Luke 14:26	John 11:3	

sister-in-law = 0 (sister-in-law = 0)

sisters-in-law = 0 (brothers-in-law = 0)

wife = 33 (husband = 9)

Matt. 1:6	Matt. 1:20	Matt. 1:24	Matt. 5:31	Matt. 5:32
Matt. 14:3	Matt. 18:25	Matt. 19:3	Matt. 19:5	Matt. 19:9
Matt. 19:10	Matt. 22:28	Matt. 27:19	Mark 6:17	Mark 6:18
Mark 10:2	Mark 10:7	Mark 10:11	Mark 12:19	Mark 12:23
Luke 1:5	Luke 1:13	Luke 1:18	Luke 1:24	Luke 3:19
Luke 8:3	Luke 14:26	Luke 16:18	Luke 17:32	Luke 18:29
Luke 20:28	Luke 20:33	John 19:25		

wives = 1 (husbands = 1)

Matt. 19:8

woman = 57 (man = 270)

Matt. 5:28	Matt. 5:32	Matt. 9:20	Matt. 9:22	Matt. 13:33
Matt. 15:22	Matt. 15:28	Matt. 22:27	Matt. 26:7	Matt. 26:10
Mark 5:25	Mark 5:33	Mark 7:25	Mark 7:26	Mark 12:22
Mark 14:3	Luke 7:37	Luke 7:39	Luke 7:44	Luke 7:50
Luke 8:43	Luke 8:47	Luke 10:38	Luke 11:27	Luke 13:11
Luke 13:12	Luke 13:16	Luke 13:21	Luke 15:8	Luke 16:18
Luke 20:32	Luke 20:33	Luke 22:57	John 2:4	John 4:7
John 4:9	John 4:11	John 4:15	John 4:17	John 4:19
John 4:21	John 4:25	John 4:27	John 4:28	John 4:42
John 8:3	John 8:4	John 8:9	John 8:10	John 16:21
John 18:16	John 18:17	John 19:26	John 20:13	John 20:15

women = 21 (men = 25)

Matt. 11:11	Matt. 14:21	Matt. 15:38	Matt. 24:41	Matt. 27:55
Matt. 28:5	Mark 15:40	Mark 15:41	Luke 1:42	Luke 7:28
Luke 8:2	Luke 12:45	Luke 17:35	Luke 23:27	Luke 23:49
Luke 23:55	Luke 24:5	Luke 24:10	Luke 24:22	Luke 24:24
John 8:5				

*Words translated to identify females in the Gospels of the New Revised Standard Version of the Bible (NRSV), according to macBible 3.0

may have known what certain women did, but most often we do not know what they said. Doctor of Philosophy, Carla Ricci, researches and writes on women in the history of the church and in her book *Mary Magdalene and Many Others: Women who followed Jesus,* she addresses the subjects of language and the silence of and about women in the Gospels:

> The critical analysis that can be made of the texts to reveal their patriarchal and androcentric language-structure-conception shows, then, as a prime element, the *absence* of women and the *silence* applied, generally if not completely, to them. This is a silence that is sometimes explicitly declared, thereby providing clear proof of the denial to which women were subjected.

On the other hand, we may conjecture that the Gospel writers were not in denial about women, but were in the process of making a dramatic change in their view of women. In several instances the Gospel writers did document the encounters of women with Jesus, often in terms of dialogue. One women who was given a voice in the Gospels had the longest of all the recorded dialogues with Jesus. She has been called the Samaritan Woman at the Well. Her dialogue and the story of her part in evangelizing her entire town are expanded upon in Chapter Two of this book.

Chapter Three contains the account of the Caught Adulteress. While the male characters in her story have control not only of her physically, but also of the dialogue that pertains to her, eventually she is given the opportunity to speak. In brief reply to the final question of Jesus, she verbalizes her observation that none of her accusers have remained, but we never know her name, her thoughts, her feelings, or her outcome.

However, several exchanges took place between Jesus and Martha of Bethany, as examined in Chapter Four. She initiated the first of their recorded dialogue. Their second encounter is the focus of our discussion.

Again, the dialogue is absent between the Hemorrhaging Woman and Jesus, as recounted in Chapter Five. We are told her story without the dialogue between her and Jesus. But what she said to herself is a valuable insight into her need and faith.

The Canaanite/Syro-Phoenician Woman of Chapter Six shouted after Jesus until he stopped to talk with her. They exchanged several rounds of dialogue, as record in the Gospels. We see her through her intelligent, tactful, and cleaver words.

Mary of Bethany is the subject of Chapter 7. Her life of reverence at the feet of Jesus is highly praised. Yet she only is given one line of dialogue, which is an exact duplication of what her sister said earlier.

Finally, in Chapter 8 all scriptures including Mary Magdalene are presented. While she had a long-lasting relationship with Jesus, we do not hear her voice in the Gospels until after the resurrection.

But a lack of recorded dialogue between Jesus and the women in the Gospels does not mean that the women did not speak or were not present or active around Jesus or in his ministry. Women may not have been mentioned because there was nothing unusual or noteworthy in their presence, participation, words, or behaviors. This idea does not diminish women, but it does remind us that the words and deeds of women go unnoticed and are viewed as normal unless they deviate from the expected, even today. Then as now, too often women worked, cleaned, gave, and served everyone around them without being noticed.

Virtues Reflection: Overview

The women around Jesus are included in the scriptures for a variety of reasons. Some of the reasons are clearer than others. Here we will consider three reasons.

First, there were women around Jesus who displayed developed virtues to be admired and emulated. One such woman was, Mary of Bethany. She displayed her developed virtue of *reverence* when she anointed Jesus with her costly ointment.

Second, there were women around Jesus who displayed the need to exercise their developed virtues. Martha is a woman who displayed the need to exercise one of her developed virtues. On one occasion when she was entertaining Jesus in her home Martha did not exercise her developed virtues of *harmony, patience,* and *service* when she complained about her sister's neglect in helping Martha prepare and serve. Later, on the occasion of Mary of Bethany's anointing of Jesus six days before his last Passover, Martha used her developed virtues as she served without complaint.

Third, there were women around Jesus who displayed the need for further development of the virtues they had. The Caught Adulteress is one example of a woman who had the need for further development of her virtues. Among the virtues she needed to develop were *purity, faithfulness, self-control,* and *trustworthiness.* With the further development and exercise of these virtues, in particular, she would not commit adultery.

As you read, ponder, and discuss the stories of the women around Jesus, you can begin your own list of womanly virtues. [The *Virtues Reflection* and *Focus Virtues* on the next two pages may be reproduced.]

Virtues Reflection

As you read the stories in the scriptures of the women around Jesus, you may come away with more questions than answers. For a number of reasons there is a lack of information regarding most female encounters retold in the Bible. Therefore, you may want to use the following as a technique to dig more deeply into the thoughts, emotions, actions, and reactions of a particular woman around Jesus. It is only when we relate to a Bible character that we can gain the full impact of that person's encounter with the Lord. In many cases, the full impact will unfold as we ponder and explore our own questions relating the Bible encounter to our own circumstances. Before answering the following questions, read all scripture references relating to the particular Bible woman and her encounter with Jesus.

1. What are the developed virtues you identify in her?

2. Which one of the developed virtues of this Bible woman do you most appreciate, today? Why this virtue?

3. What do you admire most about this Bible woman and/or her virtue?

4. How has this virtue been part of your life in the past or in the present?

5. How do you see this virtue or the need for it in your life, now?

6. What can you do to further develop this virtue in your life?

7. What has helped you most as a result of this study relating to this particular woman or her virtues?

Focus Virtues

affection
assertiveness
awareness
cheerfulness
-compassion
confidence
consideration
courageousness
determination
discernment
-faithfulness
-forgiveness
friendship
generosity
gentleness
godliness -
goodness
graciousness
gratitude *expression*
harmony
holiness
honor
hopefulness
humility
-joyfulness -
justice

A capable, intelligent and *virtuous* woman, who ... can find her? She is far more precious than jewels, and her value is far above rubies or pearls.

PROVERBS 31:10
AMPLIFIED BIBLE

kindness
- knowledge
-love
loyalty
meekness
mercifulness -
obedience
- patience
peacefulness
purity
purposefulness
respectfulness
- responsibility
reverence
righteousness
self-control
- service
steadfastness
tactfulness
trust
trustworthiness
truthfulness
-understanding
unity
willingness
wisdom

© 1996 Christine M. Carpenter•P.O. Box 8716•Portland•OR•97207•503/228-6003

Beliefs

34

Action Scripture

Philippians 3:7-12 *Yet whatever gains I had, these I have come to regard as loss because of Christ. More than that, I regard everything as loss because of the surpassing value of knowing Christ Jesus my Lord. For his sake I have suffered the loss of all things, and I regard them as rubbish, in order that I may gain Christ and be found in him, not having a righteousness of my own that comes from the law, but one that comes through faith in Christ, the righteousness from God based on faith. I want to know Christ and the power of his resurrection and the sharing of his sufferings by becoming like him in his death, if somehow I may attain the resurrection from the dead. Not that I have already obtained this or have already reached the goal; but I press on to make it my own, because Christ Jesus has made me his own.*

Grateful Prayer

Gracious God, we thank You for sending Your only Son, Jesus, to show us the way to You. We do want to know You and ask that You open our eyes to see Jesus and the women around Him in new and deeper ways that we can relate to our own lives, today. Help us live and share what You reveal to us in ways that will bless all those around us. In the name of Jesus we pray, AMEN.

In the Next Chapter...

the dialogue between Jesus and the Samaritan Woman at the Well scriptures and discussion questions examine the longest conversation between Jesus and anyone recorded in the Bible. Following them are sections with information about the physical surroundings of Samaria: The Place, the History of the Samaritans, The Symbolism of Water, and Marital Status which will help to understand the subjects discussed by Jesus and the Samaritan Woman at the Well. Then the Reflection section discusses a new perspective on how and why Jesus broke the stereotypes of the Samaritan Woman at the Well. Her encounter with Jesus is summarized, along with her Focus Virtue: Willingness, followed by the Virtues Reflection and discussion questions. An Action Scripture and Grateful Prayer conclude the chapter.

Chapter Two

Samaritan Woman at the Well

*It only takes one woman who has had
an encounter with Jesus
to bring an entire town to him.*

Christine M. Carpenter

> John 4:3-9 He left Judea and started back to Galilee. But he had to go through Samaria. So he came to a Samaritan city called Sychar, near the plot of ground that Jacob had given to his son Joseph. Jacob's well was there, and Jesus, tired out by his journey, was sitting by the well. It was about noon. A Samaritan woman came to draw water, and Jesus said to her, "Give me a drink." (His disciples had gone to the city to buy food.) The Samaritan woman said to him, "How is it that you, a Jew, ask a drink of me, a woman of Samaria?" (Jews do not share things in common with Samaritans.)

Why did the Samaritan woman come alone at noon to draw her water?

Why did Jesus ask the Samaritan woman for a drink?

a. He was thirsty.

b. He wanted to have a conversation with her.

c. He thought it would be rude to ignore her and he did not know what else to say.

d. Other?

Why was the Samaritan woman so quick to question Jesus?

a. She was suspicious of men, especially foreigners.

b. She wanted to understand what he really wanted from her.

c. A Jewish man who was not from her town had never spoken to her before and she wanted to talk to him.

d. Other?

John 4:10-14 Jesus answered her, "If you knew the gift of God, and who it is that is saying to you, 'Give me a drink,' you would have asked him, and he would have given you living water." The woman said to him, "Sir, you have no bucket, and the well is deep. Where do you get that living water? Are you greater than our ancestor Jacob, who gave us the well, and with his sons and his flocks drank from it?" Jesus said to her, "Everyone who drinks of this water will be thirsty again, but those who drink of the water that I will give them will never be thirsty. The water that I will give will become in them a spring of water gushing up to eternal life."

What is the gift of God that Jesus is talking about?

a. Living water.

b. The Holy Spirit.

c. Jesus, the Messiah.

d. Other?

Why did Jesus tell the Samaritan woman that he could give her living water and she would never be thirsty, again?

If you have ever experienced something like the spring of living water gushing up to eternal life, please remember briefly:

• **your surroundings at the time**

• **your emotional state at the time**

• **your feelings afterward**

John 4:15-18 The woman said to him, "Sir, give me this water, so that I may never be thirsty or have to keep coming here to draw water." Jesus said to her, "Go, call your husband, and come back." The woman answered him, "I have no husband." Jesus said to her, "You are right in saying, 'I have no husband'; for you have had five husbands, and the one you have now is not your husband. What you have said is true!"

If you were there with the Samaritan woman that day, would you have asked Jesus for the living water he offered? Why?

Why did Jesus ask the woman to go call her husband and come back?

a. He wanted to make the same offer of living water to her husband so the couple could be on an equal level, spiritually.

b. He wanted her to think about her life.

c. He knew that he could get into trouble for talking to a woman without a chaperone present.

d. Other?

What do you think were the circumstances that involved the Samaritan woman having had five husbands and now living with a man who was not her husband?

a. Divorce   b. Domestic Violence

c. Widowhood   d. Promiscuity

e. Abandonment   f. Childlessness

g. Disobedience   h. Other?

> John 4:19-24 The woman said to him, "Sir, I see that you are a prophet. Our ancestors worshiped on this mountain, but you say that the place where people must worship is in Jerusalem." Jesus said to her, "Woman, believe me, the hour is coming when you will worship the Father neither on this mountain nor in Jerusalem. You worship what you do not know; we worship what we know, for salvation is from the Jews. But the hour is coming, and is now here, when the true worshipers will worship the Father in spirit and truth, for the Father seeks such as these to worship him. God is spirit, and those who worship him must worship in spirit and truth."

How did the Samaritan woman know that Jesus was a prophet?

Why did the Samaritans worship in a different place than the Jews?

a. Each group of people worshiped closest to their homes.

b. The Samaritans believed their mountain was the Holy Mountain of God.

c. The Jews believed their mountain was the Holy Mountain of God.

d. Other?

How can you worship the Father in spirit and in truth?

John 4:25-28 The woman said to him, "I know that Messiah is coming" (who is called Christ). "When he comes, he will proclaim all things to us." Jesus said to her, "I am he, the one who is speaking to you." Just then his disciples came. They were astonished that he was speaking with a woman, but no one said, "What do you want?" or, "Why are you speaking with her?" Then the woman left her water jar and went back to the city.

How did the Samaritan Woman at the Well know that Messiah was coming?

a. She overheard the men talking about Messiah's coming.

b. Her husband used to talk with her about Messiah.

c. She heard the Priest mention it during one of the celebrations of feasts.

d. Other?

Why did Jesus tell the Samaritan woman that he was Messiah?

a. He knew no one else would.

b. God sent him to find her at the well and make sure she heard the news from Jesus.

c. He knew such a talkative person would make a good evangelist.

d. Other?

Why were the disciples so astonished that Jesus was talking with a woman?

> John 4:29-30, 39-43 She said to the people, "Come and see a man who told me everything I have ever done! He cannot be the Messiah, can he?" They left the city and were on their way to him. Many Samaritans from that city believed in him because of the woman's testimony, "He told me everything I have ever done." So when the Samaritans came to him, they asked him to stay with them; and he stayed there two days. And many more believed because of his word. They said to the woman, "It is no longer because of what you said that we believe, for we have heard for ourselves, and we know that this is truly the Savior of the world." When the two days were over, he went from that place to Galilee.

Why did the Samaritan woman leave her water-pot and go to town to tell the people about Jesus?

Why did Jesus stay with the Samaritans for two days?

What did Jesus say during the two days with the Samaritans that made them believe that he was truly the Savior of the world?

Do you believe that Jesus is truly the Savior of the world? Why?

Samaria: The Place

When the Hebrews entered the Promised Land the inheritance of the tribes of Ephraim and Manasseh consisted of what became Samaria. Samaria is located approximately forty-three miles north of Jerusalem, extending from the Mediterranean to the Jordan, and from the mountain mass of Gilboa and Mount Ephraim and the ridge of Carmel.

Samaria was the geographical center of Palestine. Ancient roads brought travelers from all directions, through Samaria's rich farm lands. While the network of roads exposed the Samaritans to the diversity and advances going on in other parts of the world, the same network of roads exposed the Samaritans to invasion.

The physical beauty of Samaria was due in part to its well-watered condition. Prolific olive orchards blanketed the slopes of its mountains. Cultivated vineyards enhanced the views from its glorious mountains. Samaria's inhabitants populated prosperous towns and enjoyed the fruits of the land as well as the beauty that God and man created surrounding Samaria.

The capital city was erected on the top of a 400 foot hill of Samaria. Archaeologists have unearthed three layers of history revealing the magnificence created by Samaria's builders, Kings Omri, Ahab, and Jehu, from about 876 BC to 744 BC. During the first century BC Herod created the best of what remains. At some points, the fortified walls are 33 feet thick. Ivories, carved relief, and gold inlay were all part of the decorations and furniture found by archeologists. The artifacts date back to the 9th century BC. The rounded towers on the acropolis have been dated to the Hellenistic era, around 324 BC, by archaeologist J.W. Crowfoot.

History of the Samaritans

A United Kingdom Divides

After the Patriarchs and Judges, about 1050 BC, the Hebrew people entered the time of Kings. The Hebrew nation was initially a united kingdom under King Saul, King David, and King Solomon. About 931 BC the kingdom divided into the southern kingdom of Judah and the northern kingdom of Israel.

The division occurred as a result of a dispute between Solomon's successor, his son King Rehoboam, and King Jeroboam who had been living in exile in Egypt after a failed plot to kill Solomon. When Rehoboam refused to comply with Jeroboam's demands, the king of Egypt, Sheshonk I (also called Shishak), supported Jeroboam by invading and plundering Rehoboam's kingdom and despoiling the Temple at Jerusalem. The people and the kingdom were divided politically.

Jeroboam I became king of the northern parts of the old kingdom which became known as the Kingdom of Israel. Tradition says that the Kingdom of Israel included 10 of the 12 tribes. Rehoboam remained king over the 300 square miles of Judah and Benjamin, which became the secondary power as the southern kingdom, known as the Kingdom of Judah.

Samaria is Established

Samaria's beginnings date back to the reign of Israel's King Omri (876-869 BC) who established the capital of the northern kingdom on a hill overlooking a main road to Jerusalem. During King Omri's reign, Israel was a major power in the region and a time of peace ensued. But the peace was short-lived. Assyria grew to a dominant position in the Middle East, invading and conquering Israel in the 8th century BC. The fortified city of Samaria held out against the Assyrian siege on their city until 722-721 BC.

With the northern kingdom of Israel destroyed, the Assyrians captured the wealthy, the leaders, the artisans, and the skilled to take them back to Assyrian domains. By deporting approximately 27,290 of the more influential and powerful people, the national consciousness and cohesion was compromised. The people relocated in the deportation of Israel's inhabitants have since been referred to as the Lost Tribes of Israel. Only the poor or undesirables were left. Soon Samaria was repopulated by foreigners who adopted the Hebrew religion. These emigrants from Mesopotamia intermarried with the remnant of Israel and became known as Samaritans.

Judah also Falls

Judah, on the other hand, maintained its identity during the next century. Over time, the Assyrians lost power to the Egyptians. Then the Egyptians lost to the Babylonian Empire of the Chaldeans. Defiant Jerusalem was conquered by Nebuchadnezzar II, ruler of Chaldea, in 598 BC.

In much the same way as with Israel's capture and deportation, Judah's nobles, warriors, and artisans were deported to Babylon. Rebellion continued in Judah and in the late 6th century BC Nebuchadnezzar's army destroyed the Temple at Jerusalem, along with all of Judah. Some Judeans fled to Egypt, some were taken to Babylon, and only the poorest peasants and undesirables remained. Ancient Israel's political independence was virtually over, but for a brief time more than four later.

Israel and Judah Share in Exile

In exile, the people deported from Israel and the people deported from Judah came together as a thriving colony in Babylon. Scribes compiled their traditions, some of which are our Bible, today. Without temple worship, new rituals and forms of worship were devised to meet the spiritual need of the exiles. The prayer meeting and synagogue style worship were born out of this Exile.

In 539 BC Cyrus the Great of Persia conquered the Babylonians. Cyrus emancipated the Jews a year later. Zerubbabel was chosen to lead the first Exiles—about 42,000 people—back to Jerusalem. Zerubbabel was born in captivity, his name meaning "begotten in Babylon." He was the grandson of Jehoiachin, a captive king of Judah.

Judah Returns Home and Rebuilds the Temple

Faced with the utter devastation of their country in ruins, despair ensued. First, Zerubbabel and the High Priest Joshua set up an altar and kept the feasts. Then the foundations of the temple were laid. But for the following 15 years virtually no activity took place toward rebuilding the temple. Eventually, the prophets Haggai and Zechariah encouraged the people to pursue spiritual life as their ultimate goal.

Over time, the Jews, as Judah would now be called, returned to the enormous task of rebuilding the Temple at Jerusalem. They were not without their opponents. However, the prophets kept persisting in their spiritual call. As it is called, Zerubbabel's Temple was completed in 516 BC. Jewish tradition measures the true end of the Babylonian exile to this date of the temple's completion.

The Jews Rebuff the Samaritans Permanently

It was over the rebuilding of the Temple at Jerusalem that the Jews and Samaritans had the rift that made permanent their animosity. To begin with, Samaritans were looked down on by Jews, dating back to the fall of Samaria. Because of the deportation of the leadership of the 10 tribes, the remnant of Israel not deported intermarried with foreigners who repopulated Samaria.

Some sources, even today, speak disparagingly about Samaritans. For example, the *Encyclopedia of Bible Life* says:

> We find ourselves always thankful when we have motored safely through this pass, despite its temptations to halt again at the oldest Samaritan synagogue, which is tended by a fast-vanishing company of the "mongrel" race centered in Samaria after the Exile.

Ancient Jewish attitude and sentiment toward the Samaritans escalated into a full blown schism when the Samaritans wanted to help rebuild the temple. Because they were of mixed descent, the Samaritans were barred from participating in the work. Further, Ezra and Nehemiah, the prophets of the day, forbid Samaritans to present votive or freewill offerings in the Temple at Jerusalem. In addition, because the Samaritans were not of the orthodox Hebrew standards of racial and religious purity, they were not allowed to buy large cattle or unmovable property. Nor could a Samaritan marry a Jew or circumcise a Jew. The intention of Ezra and Nehemiah's religious code was to keep interracial Samaritans from having any dealings with one-hundred percent Jews. It did not matter that Samaritans worshiped the same God as the Jews, in the same way, with the same fervor. Also, Samaritans had not entirely driven out all foreign deities from their land—because they had married foreigners over the years. But hatred and disdain for the Samaritans was more racially based than any fundamental difference of religion practiced by the Jews, according to *Eerdmans' Handbook to the Bible.*

Samaritans Get and Lose Their Own Temple

So, after being rebuffed by the Jerusalem Jews and without access to the only temple they had known, in Jerusalem,the Samaritans built their own temple in Samaria within a century and a half. *Harper's Bible Dictionary* says that it may have been Alexander the Great of Macedon, on his campaign through Palestine, who gave permission to the Samaritans to build their temple. Or their temple may have been built much earlier. In any case, the Jews rejection of the heretical Samaritans was sealed when a temple was built on Mount Gerizim, overlooking Shechem.

In 128 BC, the Jewish king, Maccabean John Hyrcanus destroyed the Samaritan temple. The Samaritans never rebuilt their temple on Mount Gerizim, but continue to confirm the sanctity of Mount Gerizim as God's chosen holy mountain by celebrating high holy days upon the mount. Samaritans assert that Mount Gerizim is where the Shekinah (glory of God shown) originated and will return in the second kingdom (Deuteronomy 12:29).

In addition, the Samaritan Pentateuch, written in the Phoenician alphabet not used since 200 BC, is still used today. The Samaritan Pentateuch is an older text of the first five books of the Bible than today's Jewish Torah.

The Symbolism of Water

The Samaritan woman met Jesus at Jacob's well. While the water there was drawn from a deep well and came up clean, clear, and cool, it was not the living water that forever quenches thirst for the things of this world. Jesus talked to the Samaritan woman of living water because he knew that from the beginning, Israel was aware of the significance of water.

Without water, the crops would not grow, the livestock would not survive, and the people would perish. Water came as God's bless in the form of a river to flow through the land. Water came as God's blessing in the form of rain falling from heaven. Water came as God's blessing in the form of a spring gushing forth, sometimes from a rock. Water came as God's blessing in the form of a well dug deep.

Deuteronomy 11 declares rain as one way God rewarded or punished. The early and late rain in its season were rewards from God. Withholding the rain was one way God demonstrated displeasure toward the actions of people. Without the rain, the water supply would be quickly exhausted and life would be lost.

After God created the heavens and the earth and all that is in them, God did not leave creation high and dry. One of the first things God did was to provide the basis for all life—water—for creation, as recorded in Genesis 2:

> *...the LORD God planted a garden in Eden...A river flows out of Eden to water the garden, and from there it divides and becomes four branches... Pishon... Gihon... Tigris... Euphrates.*

Continuing the plan for sustaining all life, the final chapter of the New Testament, Revelation 22, shows us:

...the river of the water of life, bright as crystal, flowing from the throne of God and of the Lamb through the middle of the street of the city. On either side of the river is the tree of life with its twelve kinds of fruit, producing its fruit each month; and the leaves of the tree are for the healing of the nations."

God has provided rivers to water plantings from Genesis to Revelations—from the beginning and beyond the end.

In the *Encyclopedia of Bible Life* by Madeleine S. Miller and J. Lane Miller, the authors note that ancient people said, "Where there is a spring, there let us build an altar." The book of Joshua contains many references to springs in the names of the towns recorded. Often the 'en' or 'ain' beginnings of words indicate the presence of a water source.

Deuteronomy 8:6-7 reminds the people that God will provide various forms of water for their good, therefore, they should obey God.

Therefore keep the commandments of the LORD your God, by walking in his ways and by fearing him. For the LORD your God is bringing you into a good land, a land with flowing streams, with springs and underground waters welling up in valleys and hills...

Numbers 21:16 is an example of the LORD showing the people that God is the giver of water in the form of a well.

From there they continued to Beer; that is the well of which the LORD said to Moses, "Gather the people together, and I will give them water."

In addition to providing for their physical need for water, God also provided for the spiritual use of water. The symbolic ritual of spiritual cleansing by water is recorded in Numbers 19:20:

Any who are unclean but do not purify themselves, those persons shall be cut off from the assembly, for they have defiled the sanctuary of the LORD. Since the water for cleansing has not been dashed on them, they are unclean.

However, water goes beyond necessity to nicety. Hosts would offer visitors and guests water to refresh their weary feet. In Genesis 18:4, Abram did so with his angelic company on their way to Sodom. Even Jesus took basin in hand at the last supper and washed the feet of his disciples, as found in John 13:4-14. In 1Timothy 5:10 the Apostle Paul advises Timothy of the requirements for an older woman to become a leader in the church, among which is washing the feet of the saints. This form of hospitality was not only respectful and comforting, but symbolic. Just as the physical act of washing the feet demonstrated the humility of both the one washing and the one submitting to being washed, so the water used symbolized an immersion in the basic element of God's life giving and life sustaining provision.

Marital Status

Marriage

Marriages of the time and local of the Samaritan Woman at the Well were arranged by parents. It was a daughter's duty to marry whomever her father chose for her. It was understood by all parties that the wife would become a working asset to her husband, therefore the bride's father could command a price for her, which the groom and his family would be willing to pay. This was known as "The Bride Price."

The betrothal began when the payment of the mohar (The Bride Price) was given to the father of the bride, usually in the amount of 50 shekels. But even a marriage arranged by the wisest tribal leaders or fathers did not always work for their sons and daughters. Wives could only demand a divorce if the husband did not provide her with food, clothing, shelter, and the marriage act. However, it was the husband who had the power to dispose of his wife for any reason—even burned toast. Marriages ended for a variety of reasons, including: divorce; widowhood; promiscuity; childlessness; and disobedience.

Divorce

As the accusation implies in Deuteronomy 22:13, men were sometimes sending away their wives with fabricated reasons.

> *Suppose a man marries a woman, but after going in to her, he dislikes her and makes up charges against her, slandering her by saying, "I married this woman; but when I lay with her, I did not find evidence of her virginity."*

Deuteronomy 24:1-4 made it clear that if a husband was going to send away his wife, then he also must write her out a certificate of divorce.

Suppose a man enters into marriage with a woman, but she does not please him because he finds something objectionable about her, and so he writes her a certificate of divorce, puts it in her hand, and sends her out of his house; she then leaves his house and goes off to become another man's wife. Then suppose the second man dislikes her, writes her a bill of divorce, puts it in her hand, and sends her out of his house (or the second man who married her dies); her first husband, who sent her away, is not permitted to take her again to be his wife after she has been defiled.

John Temple Bristow writes in *What Paul Really Said About Women,* that the school of Shammai interpreted Deuteronomy 24:1 to read that adultery was the only grounds for divorce, while the school of Hillel let the grounds be almost anything. Some examples cited by him include: "speaking disrespectful of his parents...spoiling his dinner with too much salt... yelling at him...if he found another woman who was more attractive than her!"

The purpose of marriage was to create a family. A husband expected his wife to produce sons for him. If this did not happen, and he was not pleased to keep her, it was understood that he had every right to divorce her and take another wife, or wives. Barrenness was considered a curse from God (Genesis 16:2; 20:18; 1Samuel 1:5) and the wife unable to produce progeny for her husband could be returned to her father's household, thus ending the marriage.

Another displeasing behavior that could result in divorce was promiscuity. The ultimate expression of promiscuity was adultery. Adultery was considered to be voluntary sexual intercourse between a married woman and any man, and not allowed under the Law. *You shall not commit adultery (*Exodus 20:14*). Neither shall you commit adultery (*Deuteronomy 5:18*).*

For a man other than her husband to have sexual intercourse with a married woman meant that the progeny she produced were questionable and may not be her husband's rightful heir. This was considered a serious act against the husband. Therefore, both adulterers were to be stoned to death according to the Law (Deuteronomy 22:21-24).

Widowhood

Deuteronomy 25:5-9 shows how difficult it was for a woman who became a widow to get free of the hand-me-down-to-my-brother-in-law or his nearest kinsman system.

> *When brothers reside together, and one of them dies and has no son, the wife of the deceased shall not be married outside the family to a stranger. Her husband's brother shall go in to her, taking her in marriage, and performing the duty of a husband's brother to her, and the firstborn whom she bears shall succeed to the name of the deceased brother, so that his name may not be blotted out of Israel. But if the man has no desire to marry his brother's widow, then his brother's widow shall go up to the elders at the gate and say, "My husband's brother refuses to perpetuate his brother's name in*

Israel; he will not perform the duty of a husband's brother to me." Then the elders of his town shall summon him and speak to him. If he persists, saying, "I have no desire to marry her," then his brother's wife shall go up to him in the presence of the elders, pull his sandal off his foot, spit in his face, and declare, "This is what is done to the man who does not build up his brother's house."

Jacob's son Judah is one example of a family patriarch remaining in control of the daughter-in-law's next husband. Had Judah not been afraid that his last son would also die in the bed of Tamar, she would have been the wife of the third son, also, as recorded in Genesis 38:6-10.

Matthew 22:24-28 gives an example of the male attitude and how far the men of Jesus' day were willing go in passing a woman from husband to husband as their right, under the law, to acquire sons:

"Teacher, Moses said, 'If a man dies childless, his brother shall marry the widow, and raise up children for his brother.' Now there were seven brothers among us; the first married, and died childless, leaving the widow to his brother. The second did the same, so also the third, down to the seventh. Last of all, the woman herself died. In the resurrection, then, whose wife of the seven will she be? For all of them had married her."

Life for the widow (and the divorced woman) was known to be difficult, as evidenced by the following scriptures:

Exodus 22:22-24 You shall not abuse any widow or orphan. If you do abuse them, when they cry out to me, I will surely heed their cry; my wrath will burn, and I will kill you with the sword, and your wives shall become widows and your children orphans.

Deuteronomy 10:17-18 For the LORD your God is God of gods and Lord of lords, the great God, mighty and awesome, who is not partial and takes no bribe, who executes justice for the orphan and the widow, and who loves the strangers, providing them food and clothing.

Isaiah 1:17d ...plead for the widow.

Another form of widowhood was abandonment. Of course, husbands left home from time to time with or without explanation, and some took longer than others to return or did not return ever. With a different slant, some husbands did not leave home, but sent their wives away. Under certain circumstances, a husband may have abandoned a wife to a life of slavery, as the following scripture tries to correct.

Deut. 21:10-14 When you go out to war against your enemies, and the LORD your God hands them over to you and you take them captive, suppose you see among the captives a beautiful woman whom you desire and want to marry, and so you bring her home to your house: she shall shave her head, pare her nails, discard her captive's garb, and shall remain in your house a full month, mourning for her father and mother; after that you may go in to her and be her husband, and she shall be your wife. But if you are not satisfied with her, you shall let her go free and not sell her for money. You must not treat her as a slave, since you have dishonored her.

Reflection

Tradition has made the Samaritan Woman at the Well an incredibly sinful, adulterous, harlot, without friends. For example, in *Clothed with the Sun,* Joyce Hollyday says that this woman was known "As a notorious sinner (she had five husbands and was living with a man to whom she was not married), she was not part of their circle."

In *Harper's Bible Dictionary,* in their section on Family, the Millers write that "Jesus spoke a stinging condemnation of a woman whose husbands were five (John 4:16-18)." The Samaritan woman who met Jesus at the well "lived for carnal pleasures" writes Edith Deen in *All of the Women of the Bible.* Glin Karssen, author of *Her Name is Woman,* writes that:

> She had given up her feminine purity for immorality, and she paid for it daily. She was an outcast without friends. This was a consequence of the kind of life she was leading.

But what does the scripture actually say? Who was this woman and what was the message Jesus had for her? Let us take a close look at this encounter, with fresh eyes and receptive hearts. Remember, this is the longest recorded conversation between Jesus and anyone in the Bible.

He left Judea and started back to Galilee. But he had to go through Samaria. So he came to a Samaritan city called Sychar, near the plot of ground that Jacob had given to his son Joseph. Jacob's well was there, and Jesus, tired out by his journey, was sitting by the well. It was about noon. A Samaritan woman came to draw water, and Jesus said to her, "Give me a drink." (His disciples had gone to the city to buy food.)

John 4:3-8

One of the most cited substantiating reasons given for the Samaritan Woman at the Well to have been a sexual sinner is the fact that she was drawing water, alone at noon, during the heat of the day. It has been conjectured, repeatedly, that she was obviously avoiding the harassment of the other women who would have been expected to mistreat her because the Samaritan woman was an adulteress harlot. Another explanation is possible.

First, she may have drawn water with the women in the morning. Perhaps she was involved in a project that consumed a lot of water. She may have needed extra water and could not wait until the cool of the late afternoon or early evening.

Second, is it possible that the Samaritan Woman at the Well did not want the companionship of other women that day? She may have wanted to be alone. Perhaps it was her way of getting some time and space to herself and her thoughts.

Third, it may be that God arranged this meeting. She may not have known why she decided to go for water at noon on that particular day. Something drew her to the well, be it a physical need or a spiritual need.

The scriptures do not tell us why she was there at that time. Unlike some Bible commentators, the scriptures omit the phrase, "as was her custom." In short, this encounter may have been as simple as a wonderful accident or as purposeful as a mission from God.

The Samaritan woman said to him, "How is it that you, a Jew, ask a drink of me, a woman of Samaria?" (Jews do not share things in common with Samaritans.)

John 4:9

The Samaritan Woman at the Well knew that Jesus was a Jew. Perhaps he was wearing his striped, fringed prayer-shall over his seamless (John 19:23-4) white tunic that would later be described as dazzling white at his transfiguration (Matthew 17:2). Whether it was the appearance of his physical stature, attire, language, or stance, she knew he was a Jew.

She also knew that Jews do not have anything to do with Samaritans. The animosity between the two had hundreds of years of precedent. In fact, Glin Karssen, author of *Her Name is Woman,* writes that it was said that "He who eats the bread of a Samaritan is like someone who eats pork." Pork was not only forbidden to eat, but Jews were forbidden to touch the carcass of a pig (Leviticus 11:7; Deuteronomy 14:8). No wonder this woman was asking why he, a Jew, would take water from her, a Samaritan.

Jesus answered her, "If you knew the gift of God, and who it is that is saying to you, 'Give me a drink,' you would have asked him, and he would have given you living water."

John 4:10

At this point it becomes obvious that Jesus is not really interested in getting a drink. Jesus dangles the mystery of living water in front of her and she bites. Now he has her hooked!

The woman said to him, "Sir, you have no bucket, and the well is deep. Where do you

> *get that living water? Are you greater than*
> *our ancestor Jacob, who gave us the well, and*
> *with his sons and his flocks drank from it?"*
>
> John 4:11-12

Jacob's well is said to be excellent, bringing up cool water from a depth of 85 feet. Today it is protected by a Greek church that has been built over it. The Samaritan woman knew that the well was deep. Therefore, noting his lack of tools to draw water from Jacob's well, she wanted to know if he was greater than Jacob? Like many of us today, she wanted to know how this mysterious living water was going to get to her.

> *Jesus said to her, "Everyone who drinks of*
> *this water will be thirsty again, but those who*
> *drink of the water that I will give them will*
> *never be thirsty. The water that I will give*
> *will become in them a spring of water*
> *gushing up to eternal life."*
>
> John 4:13-14

This mystery man does not reveal his source of living water to his potential customer, but he does continue to sell her on its benefits. First, the water he gives will quench thirst forever. Second, the water will become a gushing spring of eternal life.

> *The woman said to him, "Sir, give me this*
> *water, so that I may never be thirsty or have*
> *to keep coming here to draw water."*
>
> John 4:15

The Samaritan woman did just what Jesus suggested she should do (John 4:10). She asked Jesus for the living water he was offering. She even told him why she wanted it: 1) so she would never be thirsty, 2) so she would not have to keep coming to the well.

> *Jesus said to her, "Go, call your husband, and come back."*
>
> John 4:16

Why did Jesus ask her to return with her husband? Edith Deen in *All of the Women of the Bible* says, "If their conversation was to continue, Jesus realized that it was best for the woman's husband to be present, because it was not customary for a rabbi to hold a long conversation with a strange woman." But Jesus knew she had no husband (John 4:18). It may be that Jesus wanted her to think about the disappointments of her past so that he could show her that he, the bridegroom, understood and could satisfy her thirst for a lasting marital partner.

> *The woman answered him, "I have no husband." Jesus said to her, "You are right in saying, 'I have no husband'; for you have had five husbands, and the one you have now is not your husband. What you have said is true!"*
>
> John 4:17-18

Jesus commends her honesty by repeating that she has said what is right and true. Jesus does not condemn her for her past or present relationships with men. Jesus may have known that there was more to her story than a specific number of men.

Is it possible that the Samaritan Woman at the Well was an unfortunate victim of circumstances? She may have been disappointed by death and/or rejected by divorce or abandonment, time after time. Yes, she had five husbands, but that may not have been her fault. Yes, she was living with a man now who would not marry her, but perhaps that was her only option?

However, this man Jesus was different from the men who had used her in the past. This man was not rejecting her or her questions. Here was her opportunity to get an answer to a question she had. He knew about her and told her the truth, and perhaps he would know and tell her the truth about a spiritual question.

> *The woman said to him, "Sir, I see that you are a prophet. Our ancestors worshiped on this mountain, but you say that the place where people must worship is in Jerusalem."*
> John 4:19-20

Worship was the center of spiritual life. The Jews told the Samaritans that they were not welcome to worship at the Temple at Jerusalem. Needing to worship, the Samaritans moved their worship to Mount Gerizim. The 2,849 foot high Mount Gerizim was a holy, sacred mountain for the Samaritans, just as Mount Zion was for Jerusalem Jews. Could she have been concerned that her worship would not be accepted if she worshiped on Mount Gerizim?

> *Jesus said to her, "Woman, believe me, the hour is coming when you will worship the Father neither on this mountain nor in Jerusalem. You worship what you do not know; we worship what we know, for salvation is from the Jews. But the hour is coming, and is now here, when the true worshipers will worship the Father in spirit and truth, for the Father seeks such as these to worship him. God is spirit, and those who worship him must worship in spirit and truth."*
> John 4:21-23

63

Jesus was honest with her. He told her that it did not matter where a person worships, but what a person worships and how. Salvation was going to come from the Jews and they knew it, but the Samaritans did not know where their salvation was going to come from. Even so, that did not matter, because in the future, the true worshipers would worship God in spirit and in truth. This woman was getting a pure dose of spiritual medicine that would heal her broken life. She did not need to repent (Mark 1:14-15). She did not need to go and sin no more (John 5:14). She had done nothing of which to repent.

The woman said to him, "I know that Messiah is coming" (who is called Christ). "When he comes, he will proclaim all things to us."
                                                        John 4:25

The Samaritan woman expresses her faith in the coming Messiah. She waits for him and knows that he is coming. Best of all, she knows that when he comes he will answer all her questions.

According to Glin Karssen, author of *Her Name is Woman,* rabbis said, "It would be better that the Articles of the Law be burned than that their contents be revealed to a woman publicly." Jesus was breaking all the rules, especially talking with a Samaritan woman about spiritual matters. Now he was going to openly tell her the spiritual truth that he would not declare as openly to anyone else.

Jesus said to her, "I am he, the one who is speaking to you."
                                                        John 4:26

Jesus led Martha to a confession of his Messiahship when the two were discussing the death of Lazarus (John 11:27). Later, Jesus repeatedly asked his disciples, and finally pressed Peter, to tell him who Jesus was and only then did Peter acknowledge Jesus as Messiah (Matthew 16:16; Mark 8:29; Luke 9:20). But without a doubt, Jesus wanted the Samaritan Woman at the Well to know that she had met and was talking with her Messiah.

> *Just then his disciples came. They were astonished that he was speaking with a woman, but no one said, "What do you want?" or, "Why are you speaking with her?"*
> John 4:27

Of course they were astonished that he was speaking with a woman. Even the woman was astonished from the first sentence. Remember her reply: "How is it that you, a Jew, ask a drink of me, **a woman** of Samaria?" Why were the disciples and the woman astonished that Jesus spoke to her? *Eerdmans' Handbook to the Bible* says that a Jewish prayer contains the phrase, "Blessed art thou O Lord...who hast not made me a woman." Why was he talking to her when a male Jew did not waste his words on a woman? Joyce Hollyday, in *Clothed With the Sun,* quotes Rabbinic law, saying "Who speaks much with a woman draws down misfortune on himself, neglects the words of the law, and finally earns hell?"

> *Then the woman left her water jar and went back to the city. She said to the people, "Come and see a man who told me everything I have ever done! He cannot be the Messiah, can he?" They left the city and were on their way to him.*
> John 4:28

If this woman was such an outcast, as tradition paints her, then why did she go quickly to get her townspeople so they would not miss Messiah? Even more importantly, why would the townspeople hurry out to Jacob's well in the noonday heat on the word of a woman who was the town outcast? It is more likely that the response of the townspeople bears witness to the Samaritan Woman at the Well being a trusted and accepted member of that community.

> *Meanwhile the disciples were urging him, "Rabbi, eat something." But he said to them, "I have food to eat that you do not know about." So the disciples said to one another, "Surely no one has brought him something to eat?" Jesus said to them, "My food is to do the will of him who sent me and to complete his work. Do you not say, 'Four months more, then comes the harvest'? But I tell you, look around you, and see how the fields are ripe for harvesting. The reaper is already receiving wages and is gathering fruit for eternal life, so that sower and reaper may rejoice together. For here the saying holds true, 'One sows and another reaps.' I sent you to reap that for which you did not labor. Others have labored, and you have entered into their labor."*
>
> John 4:31-38

Jesus used the symbolism of thirsting for physical water versus thirsting for living water to make his point with the woman who came to Jacob's well for water to fill her pot. Now Jesus was using the symbolism of being satisfied from physical food versus being satisfied from spiritual food with the disciples who had gone into the city for physical food while Jesus had dined on spiritual food and water with the Samaritan Woman at the Well. Jesus went a step further, and included his disciples in the harvest of the Samaritans by delaying their trip with a two-day stay in the town of the Samaritan woman.

> *Many Samaritans from that city believed in him because of the woman's testimony, "He told me everything I have ever done." So when the Samaritans came to him, they asked him to stay with them; and he stayed there two days. And many more believed because of his word. They said to the woman, "It is no longer because of what you said that we believe, for we have heard for ourselves, and we know that this is truly the Savior of the world."*
>
> John 4:39-42

This woman heard and accepted the truth about herself. Then she heard and accepted the truth about Jesus. From the Samaritan Woman at the Well, townspeople heard and accepted the truth about Jesus. Finally, from Jesus they heard and accepted the truth about Messiah. She encountered Jesus and spoke to others. Others heard her and encountered Jesus.

This, the longest of Jesus' dialogues in the Bible, is not about sin. It is not about repentance. It is not about dos or don'ts. It is about acknowledging where a person has been, where a person is, and where a person can go through Christ Jesus.

To summarize the encounter of Jesus and the Samaritan Woman at the Well we must consider where Jesus has been and where Jesus has yet to go. Prior to his stop at the well, the ministry of Jesus focused on people and places associated with official Judaism. At the well Jesus contrasts his past ministry by giving us a preview of his eventual ministry.

In short, Jesus breaks the boundaries of tradition. Jesus speaks with a woman. Jesus, a Jew, speaks to an enemy, a Samaritan. Jesus asks a foreigner for a favor. Jesus drinks from the hand of a Samaritan. Jesus speaks about spiritual things with a woman.

What we see in this encounter is Jesus removing the traditional boundary: between man and woman; between master and servant; between chosen and rejected; between clean and unclean; between change and the status quo.

In Galatians 3:28 the Apostle Paul openly affirms to all that, *"There is no longer Jew or Greek, there is no longer slave or free, there is no longer male and female; for all of you are one in Christ Jesus."*

This is not just a simple recounting of one woman's encounter or the encounter of a whole town with Jesus. It is much more than that. The Samaritan Woman at the Well was the human vessel through which Jesus ushered in a new dimension of his ministry—of which even his own disciples were amazed and questioned.

As true as it was at noontime on that day at the well, Jesus has given not just access, but also acceptance and revelation to all women. Jesus broke more than just the gender barrier to God. Jesus broke the barriers of race, religion, and the circumstances of life. Now, all who have been prevailed upon, all who have been rejected, all who have been labeled unclean, and all who will step out of the status quo to step into a changed life in God through Christ Jesus are welcomed into the Kingdom. Now as then, an open and hungry heart is a magnet that attracts the Divine to fulfill it.

Samaritan Woman at the Well
John 4:1-42

Tired, Jesus sat alone by Jacob's well while his disciples went to the city to buy food. When a Samaritan woman came to draw water Jesus asked her for a drink. She asked him why a Jew was talking to her: 1) a woman, 2) a Samaritan. Their repartee continued several rounds as Jesus answered her questions, understood and accepted her, and revealed himself as the Messiah. When the disciples arrived, astonished to find him talking with a woman, she left her water pot and went to get the townspeople to come and meet the Messiah. They listened, believed, and followed her back to the well where they asked him to stay with them; and he stayed there two days. As a result of her willingness to go and tell others about him, many believed and later told her that Jesus was "...truly the Savior of the world."

Focus Virtue: Willingness

Restore to me the joy of your salvation,
and sustain in me a willing spirit.

Psalms 51:12

This woman went to the well for water to quench her physical thirst, and returned with living water to quench her spirit. Through the joy of her salvation she was willing to share her good news. What a joy it is to be in the presence of someone who is rejoicing in a personal encounter with Jesus. Such joy seems to go along with a willing spirit that desires to share the experience with others. When we wonder why it is difficult to share Jesus with others, perhaps we need to go again to the well and refresh ourselves in his living water that will restore the joy of our salvation and sustain our willing spirit.

I will seek to maintain a willing spirit
toward the things and people of God.

69

Virtues Reflection:
Samaritan Woman at the Well

The Samaritan Woman at the Well is a wonderful example of the possibilities of using the virtues we each have within us. Of course, admittedly, she was in the physical presence of Jesus while she was responding to their communication and spiritual interactions. Think about what that must have been like for her.

While you read, reflect, and discuss the story of the Samaritan Woman at the Well, think about which virtues you can identify in her. *(You may want to review the Focus Virtues list in Chapter One.)* After reading all the scriptures related to the Samaritan woman, spend a few minutes identifying and focusing on her developed virtues and then complete the following exercise with her in mind.

1. Which of the developed virtues of the Samaritan Woman at the Well do you most appreciate, today?

2. How have these virtues been part of your life in the past or in the present?

3. How do you see these virtues or the need for them in your life, now?

4. What can you do to further develop these virtues in your life?

5. What has helped you most about this Bible story about the Samaritan Woman at the Well, and her Focus Virtue: Willingness, or this reflection?

Action Scripture

Matthew 25:34-40 *Then the king will say to those at his right hand, 'Come, you that are blessed by my Father, inherit the kingdom prepared for you from the foundation of the world; for I was hungry and you gave me food, I was thirsty and you gave me something to drink, I was a stranger and you welcomed me, I was naked and you gave me clothing, I was sick and you took care of me, I was in prison and you visited me.' Then the righteous will answer him, 'Lord, when was it that we saw you hungry and gave you food, or thirsty and gave you something to drink? And when was it that we saw you a stranger and welcomed you, or naked and gave you clothing? And when was it that we saw you sick or in prison and visited you?' And the king will answer them, 'Truly I tell you, just as you did it to one of the least of these who are members of my family, you did it to me.'*

Grateful Prayer

Almighty God, You are a generous God. We thank You for giving us opportunities to give a stranger a cup of cold water in Your name and in remembrance of the Samaritan Woman at the Well who gave Jesus a drink and in return received living water and life everlasting from Christ Jesus. We ask that our eyes be open to our opportunities to give as unto the Lord. That our hearts be willing to do what the prompting of Your Holy Spirit leads us to do. That grace and favor be upon us to both give and receive what is needed and what would be a blessing to self and others. In Jesus' name we pray, AMEN

In the Next Chapter...

the scriptures and discussion questions begin to explore the encounter of Jesus and the Caught Adulteress. The following sections of the chapter will help to better understand what took place between Jesus and the Caught Adulteress. The section containing the history of the Temple and a diagram of it set the scene. The section containing the background of the Ten Commandments provide the context of the challenge to Jesus by the scribes and Pharisees. And the section on Stoning demonstrates the real threat to the Caught Adulteress. In the Reflection section a commentary takes the Caught Adulteress from a condemned woman to an example of what forgiveness can do for us and for others. Then her brief encounter with Jesus is summarized, as well as her Focus Virtue: Forgiveness. Concluding the chapter are the Virtues Reflection and discussion questions, along with the Action Scripture and Grateful Prayer.

Chapter Three

Caught Adulteress

Together, one woman plus Jesus Christ can make any problem leave.

Christine M. Carpenter

> John 8:2 Early in the morning he [Jesus] came
> again to the temple. All the people came to him
> and he sat down and began to teach them.

Why did Jesus come to the temple early in the morning?

a. He came to hear the reading of Torah, the Pentateuch, the first five books of the Bible.

b. He came to hear the teachings of the Mishnah, the oral commentaries on the law of Moses.

c. He came to hear the halakah, the oral law about everyday life.

d. The Jews pray three times a day and he was there for the morning prayer (shadarith).

e. Other?

What did Jesus teach all the people who came to him in the temple early in the morning?

a. It was his custom that on Monday and Thursday mornings he taught the people about the passages of Torah (Pentateuch) that were removed from the Ark of the Covenant and read from handwritten parchment scrolls to the congregation, with cantillation.

b. He taught the people about the passages from Scripture, Mishnah, and Talmud which were recited during daily morning services.

c. He taught the people about the themes for Torah readings for the festivals.

d. He taught the people about the major liturgical Torah readings which took place on sabbath and festival mornings.

e. Other?

> John 8:3-4 The scribes and the Pharisees brought a woman who had been caught in adultery; and making her stand before all of them, they said to him, "Teacher, this woman was caught in the very act of committing adultery.

If you were one of those who wanted to hear Jesus teach, how would you have felt about this indelicate interruption?

Why did scribes care about a woman who had been caught in adultery?

a. They were interpreters of the law and wanted to test Jesus regarding such specific offences.

b. They were experts in the law of Moses and were called into attendance whenever someone was accused of breaking the law of Moses.

c. Most of the scribes were also Pharisees and wanted to make a point about adultery.

d. They were leaders designing the plans to kill Jesus and were trying to trap him with words so that they could show cause that he must die.

e. Other?

What or who were the Pharisees?

a. They were the largest religious-political party in Jesus' day.

b. They were the most influential religious-political party in Jesus' day.

c. They numbered about 6,000 in all, controlled the synagogues, had great control over the general population, and wanted to discredit Jesus.

d Other?

> John 8:5 "Now in the law Moses commanded us to stone such women. Now what do you say?"

What do you think the scribes and Pharisees hoped Jesus would say?

a. "Stone her according to the law of Moses."

b. "Bring her partner in adultery with her and stone them both as it is written in the law of Moses."

c. "Forgive her and let her go if she promises not to sin in this way again."

d. "The law of Moses has been replaced by the law of Love."

e. Other?

What would you like Jesus to have said to the scribes and Pharisees?

If you were the woman caught in the act of adultery, what would you have liked Jesus to have said to the scribes and Pharisees?

a. "Leave her alone and mind your own business."

b. "How many of you actually were present when she was caught in the very act?"

c. "Why didn't you bring her partner in this sin before me along with her?"

d. "May I hear her side of the story before I pass judgment on her?"

e. Other?

> John 8:6 They said this to test him, so that they might have some charge to bring against him. Jesus bent down and wrote with his finger on the ground.

If you were the woman caught in the act of adultery, what would you have expected Jesus to say or do?

What do you think the scribes and Pharisees thought when Jesus bent down and wrote with his finger on the ground?

When Jesus stooped down and wrote on the ground, what do you think was the reaction of the people who Jesus had been teaching?

What did Jesus write on the ground?

a. The names of the scribes and Pharisees.

b. The sins of the scribes and Pharisees.

c. The names and sins of those present.

d. The Golden Rule.

e. Other?

> John 8:7-9 When they kept on questioning him, he straightened up and said to them, "Let anyone among you who is without sin be the first to throw a stone at her." And once again he bent down and wrote on the ground. When they heard it, they went away, one by one, beginning with the elders; and Jesus was left alone with the woman standing before him.

Why and for how long a time do you think Jesus wrote on the ground the first time? Why?

Why and for how long a time do you think Jesus wrote on the ground the second time? Why?

Why did Jesus say that anyone without sin could throw the first stone at the Caught Adulteress?

a. Most criminal trials required two witnesses who upon conviction of the accused would be the first to throw stones and then the rest of the community would join in.

b. Jesus knew that no one was without sin and therefore no one would qualify to begin the stoning.

c. Other?

Why did the scribes and Pharisees and all the crowd Jesus was teaching go away?

Why did the woman remain before Jesus even after all the others had left?

> John 8:10-11 Jesus straightened up and said to her, "Woman, where are they? Has no one condemned you?"
>
> She said, "No one, sir." And Jesus said, "Neither do I condemn you. Go your way, and from now on do not sin again."

Why didn't Jesus condemn the woman for breaking the law of Moses?

a. Jesus was demonstrating a higher law—the law of Love—giving forgiveness.

b. Jesus knew that forgiveness releases the forgiver from harmful thoughts that attract the negative into one's life.

c. Jesus knew that punishment—even stoning—did not stop sin or win people for God, but giving people the chance to live up to a higher standard won people to God.

d. Jesus wanted to model the spiritual law of giving and receiving—that judging and condemning even a woman caught in the act of sinning would place a person in a position to be connected with the condemned, and a target to receive judgement and condemnation.

e. Other?

Can you share a time when someone gave you forgiveness instead of punishment, and what it meant to you?

The Temple

The word *temple* comes from the Latin word for a sacred, ceremonial space, *templum*. A temple is said to be an official place of worship for one or more gods. Its structure is usually large and impressive, standing out from other architecture in the area. Such dwelling places of "the divine" are common to most societies. Originally, it is believed that a temple was a concrete way for primitive people to create a relationship with the unseen, through ritual and ceremony.

The positioning of a temple often was a strategic placement. A natural feature or phenomenon not only evoked a response in its worshipers, but also reminded them to worship. Such a feature or phenomenon may have been a holy mountain or other object of nature, the apparent traverse of the sun, or a place of divine encounter. Some anthropologists suggest that the temple was on an elevated location that seemed to lessen the distance between mortals and the heavens.

Temples have taken the forms of a plain mound of heaped-up material, to ornate and sophisticated complexes consisting of numerous buildings surrounding the central structure of the temple proper. Most temples have a special place reserved for the divine presence. Out of respect for the divine, the sanctuary where the deity abides or meets the worshiper is usually nestled deep within the rest of the temple structure and unavailable to casual visitors.

Generally present somewhere within the temple complex is an altar. It may consist of a sacred stone or a simple table upon which to perform worship. The altar is where mortal meets divine, making some kind of an action or transaction. This bonding at the altar establishes, reestablishes, or sustains the relationship.

The Tabernacle: A Foreshadow of The Temple

Before the Tabernacle in the wilderness, the Hebrews did not have an official place or ritual of worship. Soon after Moses led the children of Israel out of Egypt God gave detailed instructions for a place where God could dwell among the people and reveal to them the presence of God.

The first tabernacle was the "provisional" tabernacle called the "tent of meeting" which was set up outside the camp of the Israelites during the first part of their wilderness journey (Exodus 33:7-11; 34:34-35). Second was the "Sinaitic" tabernacle for which God gave specific, detailed instructions (Exodus, Chapters 25-40). The "Davidic" tabernacle was the third tabernacle mentioned in the Old Testament and was set up in Jerusalem to receive the Ark of the Covenant (2Samuel 6:17).

The Forgotten Temple: The House of Yahweh

When King David brought the Ark of the Covenant into Jerusalem to give it a permanent home, he may not have been planning the first temple for God. The Ark of the Covenant had previously resided at Shiloh. The town of Shiloh hosted "a house of Yahweh" which was also called a temple (1Samuel 1:7, 9, 24; 3:3).

David wanted to build a proper house, a temple, for God, but was prevented from doing so, by God (2Samuel 7:1-2). However, David did plan for the temple that would be built later. David accumulated wealth with which to build the temple building and gifts for use in the temple. After David's death, his son, King Solomon, fulfilled his father's dream and built a permanent home for the God of Israel.

The First Temple: Solomon's Temple

Solomon's Temple measured 105 feet in length, 35 feet in width, and 50 feet in height. The long building contained three successive rooms: the 15 foot vestibule, the 60 foot long holy place, and the 30 foot long most holy place. The temple rooms were entered from east to west.

Even though King David told Solomon to use the building plans he received from the Lord (1Chronicles 28:11-13, 19), the temple design was much like Syrian and Canaanite temples. In recent decades similar temples have been unearthed at Hazor, Lachish, and Tainat. Similarities between the Hebrew Temple at Jerusalem and Phoenician temples may have come about through David's friendship with King Hiram of Tyre. When Solomon set out to fulfill his father's plans, he went to Hiram for help in the building project.

Inside, the walls were cedar, the floors cypress, and much gold was inlaid throughout. The decorations were designs of cherubim, flowers, and palm trees. Doors were carved and inlaid. Two freestanding bronze pillars, 35 feet in height and nearly six feet across, were decorated with pomegranates and lily-work netting. The 30 feet square bronze altar was 15 feet in height. There were six vessels to hold 200 gallons of water each, and another to hold 10,000 gallons. It took seven years to build just the sanctuary.

Solomon's Temple was built on Mount Moriah, north of the ancient City of David. It was dedicated about 952 BC, and was the crowning achievement of Solomon's reign. In 587 BC, the Babylonians were finally successful in taking captive the people and destroying Jerusalem, burning it along with Solomon's Temple.

Zerubbabel's Temple

In 538 BC, by a decree of Cyrus, the Jews were allowed to leave Babylon and return to Jerusalem to rebuild Solomon's Temple. The rebuilding began with the temple platform which was about 100 feet square. The interior is believed to have been about the same as Solomon's Temple, but not as ornate.

The Prophets Ezra, Haggai, and Zechariah repeatedly urged the discouraged people to rebuild. Over the years they had several starts at the enormous project and never really accomplished the task. That is why Herod's Temple is called the Second Temple.

Herod's Temple

In first century BC Jerusalem, during the Roman rule of Herod the Great, the grandest of all the many buildings constructed in Palestine in classical Roman style was Herod's Temple. Wanting to gain the favor of his subjects, Herod set out to make his Hebrew subjects the biggest and best temple Jerusalem had ever seen. Herod's project to rebuild and enhance Zerubbabel's Temple began in 20 BC, taking more than 80 years to complete.

Herod added magnificent porches around the entire temple, double and triple arches as gateways, and a monumental staircase connecting the main street below to the temple.

However, as Jesus predicted, Herod's Temple would not stand for long. In AD 70 Jerusalem and its Temple were destroyed during the Jewish revolt against Roman authority. Historians give the date of the temple's destruction as the same day of the same month that the first temple, Solomon's Temple, had been destroyed over 650 years earlier.

Plan of Herod's Temple

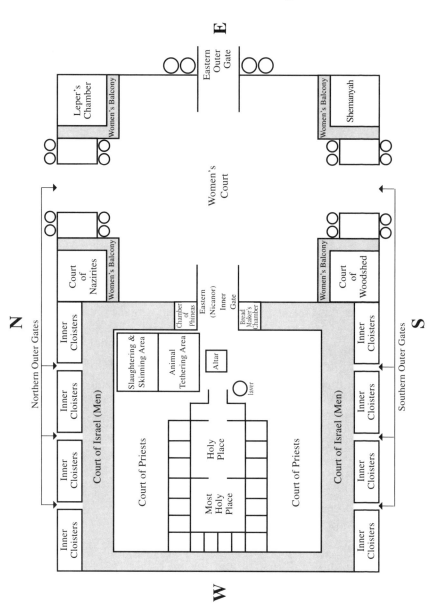

Selected Details of Herod's Temple

Temple complex stood on 1,000 by 1,500 foot rock platform made of cut stones over 15 feet long and 13 feet thick

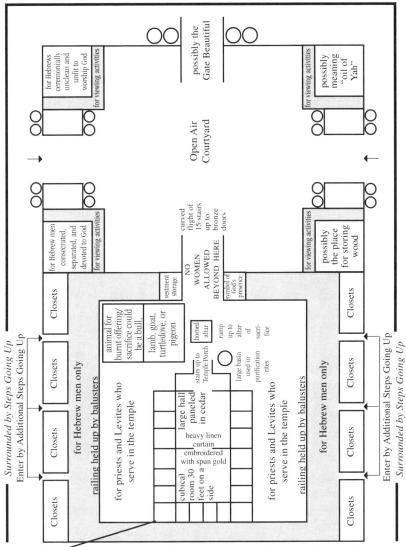

Sanctuary built of white marble stones covered with plates of heavy gold and golden spikes rising from the roof to about 165 feet.

The Temple Mount Today

Excavations on the Temple Mount since 1968 have uncovered traces of what are believed to have been other structures around the Temple. For example, today's visitors to the famous Western (Wailing) Wall, part of the original wall that once surrounded Herod's Temple, are standing above a former thoroughfare. This public access running along the base of the walls of Herod's Temple was lined with shops.

Also uncovered are stones from the southwest tower. One of the blocks bears the inscription, "the place of trumpeting." It is in the location where a priest would have announced to the city the beginning of the sabbath by blowing the shophar, a ceremonial ram's horn.

In addition, gates leading through tunnels into the large courtyard around the temple have been redis-covered on the southern side of the temple.

Also remaining is the rock platform the temple was built upon. Its foundation was 1,000 by 1,500 feet. This foundation was made of cut stones over 15 feet long and 13 feet thick. They are held in place by their original 100-foot-high retaining walls.

But the most exciting discovery resulting from excavations on the Temple Mount still waits to be confirmed. In 1982 Rabbi Yehuda Getz, chief rabbi of the Western Wall, was leading an excavation team who were looking for the original stones of Solomon's Temple. The team was 57 feet underground when a stone was moved, revealing what they describe as one of the main entrances to Solomon's Temple. How-ever, when the team returned the next day they found that the Muslims had sealed off the tunnel with a concrete wall and forbid further access.

The Ten Commandments

Exodus 31:18 says that, *When God finished speaking with Moses on Mount Sinai, he gave him the two tablets of the covenant, tablets of stone, written with the finger of God.*

Harper's Bible Dictionary by Madeleine S. Miller and J. Lane Miller says that the Ten Commandments were initially spoken by God and later inscribed on the Tables of the Law. They believe that the two stone tablets had writing on both sides. Moses made a second set of tablets after destroying the originals in a rage of anger when he descended Mount Sinai and found the people worshiping a golden calf. It is believed that the second set of tablets were put into the Ark of the Covenant.

Ancient Secrets of the Bible authors Charles E. Sellier and Brian Russel write that Gene Faulstich, a chronologist with the Chronology-History Research Institute in Spencer, Iowa says that:

> We're able to precisely date 116 major events connected with this account [referring to the Exodus story]....The Israelites first heard the Ten Commandments spoken verbally by the Lord from Mount Sinai on May 28, 1461 BC.

Further, Sellier and Russel write that Egyptologist and archaeological writer Emmanuel Anati concludes from his thirty years of experience excavating ruins that the Ten Commandments were:

> ...an engraving on a rectangular stone tablet with two ear-like shapes on top. Lines divided the tablet into ten squares. The Bible is not explicit as to what was engraved on

the tablets containing the Ten Commandments. Nowhere are we told whether they
were engraved with a script, either ancient
Semitic or Egyptian, or with symbols, or with
simple markings. Any script would probably
have been unintelligible to the majority of
the Israelites fleeing from Egyptian slavery.

Exodus 20:1: Then God spoke all these words: Exodus
20:2: *I am the LORD your God, who brought you out
of the land of Egypt, out of the house of slavery;*

1. Exodus 20:3: *You shall have no other gods before
   me.*

2. Exodus 20:4: *You shall not make for yourself an
   idol, whether in the form of anything that is in
   heaven above, or that is on the earth beneath, or
   that is in the water under the earth.* Exodus 20:5:
   *You shall not bow down to them or worship them;
   for I the LORD your God am a jealous God,
   punishing children for the iniquity of parents, to
   the third and the fourth generation of those who
   reject me,* Exodus 20:6: *but showing steadfast love
   to the thousandth generation of those who love
   me and keep my commandments.*

3. Exodus 20:7: You shall not make wrongful use of
   the name of the LORD your God, for the LORD
   will not acquit anyone who misuses his name.

4. Exodus 20:8-11: *Remember the sabbath day, and
   keep it holy. Six days you shall labor and do all
   your work. But the seventh day is a sabbath to the
   LORD your God; you shall not do any work —
   you, your son or your daughter, your male or
   female slave, your livestock, or the alien resident
   in your towns. For in six days the LORD made*

heaven and earth, the sea, and all that is in them, but rested the seventh day; therefore the LORD blessed the sabbath day and consecrated it.

5. Exodus 20:12: *Honor your father and your mother, so that your days may be long in the land that the LORD your God is giving you.*
6. Exodus 20:13: *You shall not murder.*
7. Exodus 20:14: **You shall not commit adultery.**
8. Exodus 20:15: *You shall not steal.*
9. Exodus 20:16: *You shall not bear false witness against your neighbor.*
10. Exodus 20:17: *You shall not covet your neighbor's house; you shall not covet your neighbor's wife, or male or female slave, or ox, or donkey, or anything that belongs to your neighbor.*

"Most of the apodictic laws, those written in direct address such as the Ten Commandments, were written to and for males," writes Alice Ogden Bellis, author of *Helpmates, Harlots, and Heroes.* Continuing, she points out that, "Thou shalt not covet thy neighbor's wife" is clearly not addressed to women." In addition, "The casuistic laws similarly began usually with the phrase 'If a man [male] does X . . .' "

Adding emphasis to the Ten Commandments, known as the law of Moses, the theme of sexual misconduct is further addressed in the following scripture passages:

Deuteronomy 22:22: *If a man is caught lying with the wife of another man, both of them shall die, the man who lay with the woman as well as the woman. So you shall purge the evil from Israel.*

Leviticus 19:20-22: *If a man has sexual relations with*

a woman who is a slave, designated for another man but not ransomed or given her freedom, an inquiry shall be held. They shall not be put to death, since she has not been freed; but he shall bring a guilt offering for himself to the LORD, at the entrance of the tent of meeting, a ram as guilt offering. And the priest shall make atonement for him with the ram of guilt offering before the LORD for his sin that he committed; and the sin he committed shall be forgiven him.

Deuteronomy 22:23-24: *If there is a young woman, a virgin already engaged to be married, and a man meets her in the town and lies with her, you shall bring both of them to the gate of that town and stone them to death, the young woman because she did not cry for help in the town and the man because he violated his neighbor's wife. So you shall purge the evil from your midst.*

Deuteronomy 22:25-27: *But if the man meets the engaged woman in the open country, and the man seizes her and lies with her, then only the man who lay with her shall die. You shall do nothing to the young woman; the young woman has not committed an offense punishable by death, because this case is like that of someone who attacks and murders a neighbor. Since he found her in the open country, the engaged woman may have cried for help, but there was no one to rescue her.*

Deuteronomy 22:28-29: *If a man meets a virgin who is not engaged, and seizes her and lies with her, and they are caught in the act, the man who lay with her shall give fifty shekels of silver to the young woman's father, and she shall become his wife. Because he violated her he shall not be permitted to divorce her as long as he lives.*

Numbers 5:11-31: *The LORD spoke to Moses, saying: Speak to the Israelites and say to them: If any man's wife goes astray and is unfaithful to him, if a man has had intercourse with her but it is hidden from her husband, so that she is undetected though she has defiled herself, and there is no witness against her since she was not caught in the act; if a spirit of jealousy comes on him, and he is jealous of his wife who has defiled herself; or if a spirit of jealousy comes on him, and he is jealous of his wife, though she has not defiled herself; then the man shall bring his wife to the priest.*

And he shall bring the offering required for her, one-tenth of an ephah of barley flour. He shall pour no oil on it and put no frankincense on it, for it is a grain offering of jealousy, a grain offering of remembrance, bringing iniquity to remembrance. Then the priest shall bring her near, and set her before the LORD; the priest shall take holy water in an earthen vessel, and take some of the dust that is on the floor of the tabernacle and put it into the water.

The priest shall set the woman before the LORD, dishevel the woman's hair, and place in her hands the grain offering of remembrance, which is the grain offering of jealousy. In his own hand the priest shall have the water of bitterness that brings the curse. Then the priest shall make her take an oath, saying, "If no man has lain with you, if you have not turned aside to uncleanness while under your husband's authority, be immune to this water of bitterness that brings the curse. But if you have gone astray while under your husband's authority, if you have defiled yourself and some man other than your husband has had intercourse with you," —let the priest make the woman

*take the oath of the curse and say to the woman —
"the LORD make you an execration and an oath
among your people, when the LORD makes your
uterus drop, your womb discharge; now may this water
that brings the curse enter your bowels and make your
womb discharge, your uterus drop!" And the woman
shall say, "Amen. Amen."*

*Then the priest shall put these curses in writing, and
wash them off into the water of bitterness. He shall
make the woman drink the water of bitterness that
brings the curse, and the water that brings the curse
shall enter her and cause bitter pain. The priest shall
take the grain offering of jealousy out of the woman's
hand, and shall elevate the grain offering before the
LORD and bring it to the altar; and the priest shall
take a handful of the grain offering, as its memorial
portion, and turn it into smoke on the altar, and
afterward shall make the woman drink the water.*

*When he has made her drink the water, then, if she
has defiled herself and has been unfaithful to her
husband, the water that brings the curse shall enter
into her and cause bitter pain, and her womb shall
discharge, her uterus drop, and the woman shall
become an execration among her people.*

*But if the woman has not defiled herself and is clean,
then she shall be immune and be able to
conceive children. This is the law in cases of jealousy,
when a wife, while under her husband's authority, goes
astray and defiles herself, or when a spirit of jealousy
comes on a man and he is jealous of his wife; then he
shall set the woman before the LORD, and the priest
shall apply this entire law to her. The man shall be
free from iniquity, but the woman shall bear her
iniquity.*

Stoning

Stoning was one form of capital punishment used by the Hebrews, by God's instruction. Stoning was a community affair. Everyone could participate in hurling sharp, jagged stones at the condemned. However, there was a prescribed protocol to be followed, as instructed in Deuteronomy 17.

On the evidence of two or three witnesses the death sentence shall be executed; a person must not be put to death on the evidence of only one witness. The hands of the witnesses shall be the first raised against the person to execute the death penalty, and afterward the hands of all the people. So you shall purge the evil from your midst. If a judicial decision is too difficult for you to make between one kind of bloodshed and another, one kind of legal right and another, or one kind of assault and another —any such matters of dispute in your towns — then you shall immediately go up to the place that the LORD your God will choose, where you shall consult with the Levitical priests and the judge who is in office in those days; they shall announce to you the decision in the case.

The following examples show that the Law commanded that specific offences be punished by stoning to death.

• Anyone who touched the sacred mountain (Mount Sinai) was to be stoned to death (Exod. 19:13).

• Male and female mediums and wizards were to be stoned to death (Lev. 20:27).

- Blasphemers and cursors of God were stoned to death (Lev. 24:23).
- Disobeying any instructions from the LORD was grounds for being stoned to death (Josh. 7:25).
- Anyone who resided in Israel and found working on the sabbath was to be stoned to death (Num. 15:35).
- Anyone trying to turn away the Israelites from the LORD was to be stoned to death (Deut. 13:10).
- Anyone in any Israelite town caught worshiping other gods was to be stoned to death (Deut. 17:5).
- Children who were stubborn and rebellious or gluttons and drunkards were to be stoned to death (Deut. 21:21).
- In the case of a young woman marrying and on her wedding night not being able to prove her virginity, the men of her town were to stone her to death (Deut. 22:21).
- Both the man and woman caught in adultery were to be stoned to death (Deut. 22:24).

Not only people were put to death by stoning, but animals, also. If an ox gored a man or a woman to death, the ox was to be stoned to death (Exod. 21:28). Fortunately for the owner of the ox, he was not held liable for the goring death of the man or woman. Unfortunately for the owner, no one could eat the ox meat, so the owner incurred financial loss as a result of his animal's misconduct. However, if the ox had a history of goring, and its owner was warned but had not restrained it, both the ox and its owner were stoned (Exod. 21:29). In the case of the ox killing a male or female slave, the owner payed the slave-owner thirty shekels of silver, and the ox was stoned (Exod. 21:32).

Reflection

Before we can reflect on any Bible story we must first put that story in context. However, placing in context the story of the woman caught in adultery and brought before Jesus is not just difficult, but virtually impossible as it is missing from the earliest Greek manuscripts of the Gospel according to John. When her story does appear in later translations it is found in various places within or at the end of the text. While both Christian and scholarly traditions believe the story to be authentic and accurate, the question of just where it belongs in the Bible has not been settled to everyone's satisfaction. So this story becomes an exception to the rule of context and is best studied as a stand alone passage.

The story of the Caught Adulteress begins in John 8:2 as the author tells us that it was early in the morning when Jesus went to the temple, again. Apparently it was not the first time he appeared in the temple. He may have been a regular attendee, keeping the shadarith tradition of the Jews. The Jews prayed three times a day and the morning prayer was called shadarith. It is likely that Jesus kept this tradition when he was in Jerusalem, because the scribes and Pharisees knew where to find him when they wanted to get his judgment on the Caught Adulteress.

Perhaps it was widely know that Jesus would be in the temple in the morning, because verse 2 also says that "all" the people came to Jesus and he sat and taught them. The Jewish custom was that the passages from Scripture, Mishnah, and Talmud were recited during daily morning services. Monday and Thursday mornings the passages of Torah (Pentateuch) were removed from the Ark of the Covenant and read to the congregation from handwritten parchment scrolls, accompanied by cantillation, like rhythmic musical chanting. Jesus may have been expounding upon the morning's scriptures. However, he had just begun teaching when he was interrupted.

Without invitation or regard for the teacher or his students, the scribes and the Pharisees stood a woman in front of Jesus and explained the charges against her. Then they asked Jesus if he agreed or disagreed with the law of Moses. These men were interpreters and experts in the law of Moses. They were not seeking truth or justice, but were using this woman in an attempt to trap Jesus.

But then, as now, Jesus outwitted his opponents. Rarely did Jesus give a direct answer to a question posed to him in the Gospels. Some people, today, have the same experience with answers to their questions posed to the Lord. However, then, as now, Jesus always answered in some way. That day, to the scribes and Pharisees Jesus answered both verbally and nonverbally. In silence Jesus wrote on the ground with his finger and only after the repeated questioning of the scribes and Pharisees did Jesus tell them that the one among them who had no sin could throw the first stone at the woman. Then he went back to silently writing on the ground. According to Jewish law, most criminal trials required two witnesses who upon conviction of the accused would be the first to throw stones and then the rest of the community would join in. Of course, then as now, Jesus knew that no one was without sin and therefore no one would qualify to begin the stoning of the woman.

However, the men did not leave her and Jesus alone until after Jesus wrote on the ground for the second time. Whatever he wrote on the ground must have been understood and satisfied the question, because each man left, beginning with the elders. Elders would have been the most respected leaders. What each man read, written by the finger of the Divine, may have been as simple as a sin or as complex as each man's name identified with his sin(s). The scribes and Pharisees did not stopped questioning Jesus and leave the woman with him without a reason. It is only reasonable to believe Jesus wrote something each man interpreted as a reason for leaving.

After everyone was gone, Jesus stood. He asked the woman where her accusers were and who they were who would condemn her. When she told Jesus that no one stayed to condemned her, he told her that he did not condemn her either—sending her away with instructions to refrain from sinning.

In this scenario we see Jesus faced with the facts regarding not just a sin but its required punishment. This sin was a crime committed against a man by a woman [we will not discuss where her partner in adultery was during this trial before Jesus]. Also, the man whom the crime was committed against was not just any man, he was the woman's own husband. Surely, her death was not only justified in the law, it was demanded in the heart betrayed. Yet, Jesus let her off with a warning not to do it again. Where was the justice in not punishing for a crime?

How often have we been on the giving or receiving end of a situation in our own lives that presented itself with clear-cut facts which carried a prescribed punishment. Did we give or get what we deserved? Even for a crime punishable by death, Jesus demonstrated a higher law—the law of mercy and forgiveness. If Jesus knew that he was not sent into the world to condemn, but to bring mercy and forgiveness, how can we stick to the letter of the law, condemning people? Jesus knew that punishment did not stop sin or win people for God. Now as then, people are won to God when they are given the chance to live up to a higher standard. Justice may be giving people what they deserve, but God, through Jesus Christ, introduced to us the concept and the ability to rise to a higher law—mercy and forgiveness. If we are to be like him in this world, we must learn when it is appropriate to be merciful and forgiving.

"The law is the law" attitude would have resulted in a stoning that morning. Then the Caught Adulteress would not have had an opportunity to correct her behavior. How often have we appreciated the opportunity to do better.

With God, we always have the opportunity to receive forgiveness and have a fresh start. In fact, just as Jesus demonstrated, the forgiveness is always there, even without our asking. Divine forgiveness has been given to us, but it is only when we consciously receive that forgiveness that we can begin to move past our transgression and on to a higher level of living.

That day in the Temple, Jesus helped the scribes, Pharisees, and all the crowd move past judgement and condemnation of the Caught Adulteress and on to the process of letting go of the transgression and disconnecting from the transgressor. They may not have heard the words Jesus spoke to the woman, but they had a taste of the concept and were able to leave his presence considering the possibilities of giving and receiving forgiveness.

The Caught Adulteress left the presence of Jesus knowing she was a forgiven woman. Before others leave our presence, let us send them away knowing they are not condemned and can begin anew.

Caught Adulteress
John 8:2-11

Hebrew law required both the man and woman caught in adultery to be put to death (Leviticus 20:10; Deuteronomy 22:22). However, in this case only the woman was set before the crowd as an object lesson of sin. She was brought for judgement and humiliation while her partner was never mentioned. Probably half-naked, disheveled, and required to stand facing Jesus, she waited for the impact of the first jagged rock to puncture her skin. But no one hurled anything her way. After her accusers had departed one by one beginning with the elders, without condemning her, Jesus told her that he did not condemn her either—nor should she sin in this way again.

Focus Virtue: Forgiveness

Do not judge, and you will not be judged; do not condemn, and you will not be condemned. Forgive, and you will be forgiven.

Luke 6:37

The elders and others waited eagerly for Jesus to pronounce his judgement against the woman, but Jesus delayed. Before he said a word he bent down and wrote on the ground. Then he said the person without sin should cast the first stone. He bent down again and wrote more. Was he listing names and sins, beginning with the elders? Before we cast our verbal stones at the guilty, perhaps we should go before Jesus and read what he is writing about us and our sins. When we weigh our own sins, our side of the justice scale will also fall down under the weight of our sins. Remember that we are all guilty and that we are all forgiven. Then rejoice that we have a Just Judge who will administer grace and mercy according to God's great love—and so can we.

At every opportunity I will be quick to forgive the offender.

99

Virtues Reflection:
Caught Adulteress

Again, we are reminded that the women around Jesus in the Gospels are able to teach us a variety of things. This woman, the Caught Adulteress, can teach us about virtues that are to be developed and exercised, because what we do or do not do affects our sisters, brothers, and entire community.

Today, when you read about, think on, and discuss the story of the Caught Adulteress, identify the virtues you think she needed to develop. Then identify her developed virtues that you see in her. *(You may want to review the Focus Virtues list in Chapter One.)* After reading all pertinent scriptures, take a few moments to complete the following exercise with her in mind.

1. Which virtues do you think the Caught Adulteress needed to develop?

2. Which one of the developed virtues of the Caught Adulteress do you most appreciate, today? Why?

3. How has the virtue of Forgiveness been part of your life in the past or in the present?

4. How do you see Forgiveness or the need for it in your life, now?

5. What can you do to further develop Forgiveness in your life?

6. What has been the most valuable part of this study or reflection?

Action Scripture

Luke 6:36-38 *[Jesus said,] "Be merciful, just as your Father is merciful. Do not judge, and you will not be judged; do not condemn, and you will not be condemned. Forgive, and you will be forgiven; give, and it will be given to you. A good measure, pressed down, shaken together, running over, will be put into your lap; for the measure you give will be the measure you get back."*

Grateful Prayer

Merciful God, You are a Forgiving God. You are a Just God. We thank You for accepting us even when we are caught in sin. We thank You for defending us in the presence of our accusers. We thank You for reminding us that You do not condemn us, but forgive us. We thank You for strength to resist the temptations to sin. Now we ask You to give us wisdom and understanding to give mercy and forgiveness to others and ourselves, in order that we might have another chance to do the good You desire. And we ask that we be given mercy and forgiveness so that we may do for You and others the good You desire. We pray all this in the name of Jesus, AMEN.

In the Next Chapter…

the scripture passages relating to the encounters of Jesus and Martha provide challenging concepts for the discussion questions and understanding the interactions of Jesus and Martha. Knowing the background information of the times and customs often helps to understand a person or situation. Martha may be better understood when taking into consideration the following sections of the chapter, Burial Customs and Messiah, in particular. The Reflection focuses on her interactions with Jesus and how her example can point the way to receiving a miracle. A summary of Martha's life and Focus Virtue: Friendliness are followed by the Virtues Reflection and discussion questions. An Action Scripture and Grateful Prayer conclude the chapter.

Chapter Four

Martha of Bethany

Jesus will draw out the best in every woman.

Christine M. Carpenter

> **Luke 10:38-42** Now as they went on their way, he entered a certain village, where a woman named Martha welcomed him into her home. She had a sister named Mary, who sat at the Lord's feet and listened to what he was saying. But Martha was distracted by her many tasks; so she came to him and asked, "Lord, do you not care that my sister has left me to do all the work by myself? Tell her then to help me." But the Lord answered her, "Martha, Martha, you are worried and distracted by many things; there is need of only one thing. Mary has chosen the better part, which will not be taken away from her."

About what was Martha worried and distracted?

a. She wanted everything to be perfect for Jesus.

b. She hoped to impress all her guests.

c. She thought she was missing out on something.

d. Other?

When you have guests in your home, what can worry and distract you?

What do you think Martha learned that day?

a. Not to criticize others in front of Jesus or she would be criticized, too.

b. To do what her heart tells her, not what her head thinks is right.

c. How to let go of her worries and distractions and make time with Jesus the first priority in her life.

d. Other?

> **Excerpts from John 11:1-6** Now a certain man was ill, Lazarus of Bethany, the village of Mary and her sister Martha....So the sisters sent a message to Jesus, "Lord, he whom you love is ill." But when Jesus heard it, he said, "This illness does not lead to death; rather it is for God's glory, so that the Son of God may be glorified through it." Accordingly, though Jesus loved Martha and her sister and Lazarus, after having heard that Lazarus was ill, he stayed two days longer in the place where he was.
>
> **John 11:17-20** When Jesus arrived, he found that Lazarus had already been in the tomb four days. Now Bethany was near Jerusalem, some two miles away, and many of the Jews had come to Martha and Mary to console them about their brother. When Martha heard that Jesus was coming, she went and met him, while Mary stayed at home.

Why do you think the scriptures say that Jesus loved Martha, and then referenced her sister without using her name and their dead or dying brother, Lazarus, last?

Why did Martha get up and go to meet Jesus?

a. Martha was grieving and wanted to see her beloved friend and receive his comfort.

b. Martha did not want to talk with Jesus in front of the house full of mourners.

c. Meeting Jesus on his way to her was showing her hospitality and respect for him.

d. Other?

Why did Martha go to meet Jesus without Mary?

> **John 11:21-27** Martha said to Jesus, "Lord, if you had been here, my brother would not have died. But even now I know that God will give you whatever you ask of him." Jesus said to her, "Your brother will rise again." Martha said to him, "I know that he will rise again in the resurrection on the last day." Jesus said to her, "I am the resurrection and the life. Those who believe in me, even though they die, will live, and everyone who lives and believes in me will never die. Do you believe this?" She said to him, "Yes, Lord, I believe that you are the Messiah, the Son of God, the one coming into the world."

Why did Martha talk to Jesus the way she did in John 11:21-27?

a. Martha knew Lazarus would not have died if Jesus had been with him when he was sick.

b. Martha wanted Jesus to know that she believed in the power of Jesus to ask God to restore Lazarus.

c. Martha was questioning her beliefs.

d. Martha was verifying her friendship and belief in Jesus.

e. Martha was trying to understand the concept that there is no death.

f. Other?

How had Martha come to know and believe that Jesus was the Messiah?

When did or would you say something like Martha's confession to Jesus ("Yes, Lord, I believe that you are the Messiah, the Son of God, the one [who has come] coming into the world.")?

> **John 11:28-33** When she had said this, she went back and called her sister Mary, and told her privately, "The Teacher is here and is calling for you." And when she heard it, she got up quickly and went to him. Now Jesus had not yet come to the village, but was still at the place where Martha had met him. The Jews who were with her in the house, consoling her, saw Mary get up quickly and go out. They followed her because they thought that she was going to the tomb to weep there. When Mary came where Jesus was and saw him, she knelt at his feet and said to him, "Lord, if you had been here, my brother would not have died." When Jesus saw her weeping, and the Jews who came with her also weeping, he was greatly disturbed in spirit and deeply moved.

Why did Martha go and get Mary and tell her that, "The Teacher is here and is calling for you," when the scriptures do not say Jesus was calling for Mary?

a. Jesus had told Martha to get Mary, just the way she did, but the writer thought everyone would know that without writing it twice.

b. Martha knew Jesus so well that she knew what to do and say for him.

c. Martha did not want her sister to miss being present at the resurrection of their brother.

d. Other?

Why wasn't Jesus disturbed after discussing the death of Lazarus with Martha, but was greatly disturbed when he saw Mary and the mourning Jews weeping? What was different between the two encounters?

> **John 11:34-39** He said, "Where have you laid him?" They said to him, "Lord, come and see." Jesus began to weep. So the Jews said, "See how he loved him!" But some of them said, "Could not he who opened the eyes of the blind man have kept this man from dying?" Then Jesus, again greatly disturbed, came to the tomb. It was a cave, and a stone was lying against it. Jesus said, "Take away the stone." Martha, the sister of the dead man, said to him, "Lord, already there is a stench because he has been dead four days."

Why did Jesus weep?

a. He was sorry he had not come in time to heal Lazarus before he died.

b. He realized that no one understood resurrection—life after death.

c. He just realized that the people did not know that he was Messiah.

d. It was a natural reaction to the weeping going on around him.

e. He was so hurt that Mary and the other weeping folk did not know and believe that Jesus had come to raise Lazarus from the dead.

f. Other?

Why didn't Martha weep when everyone else was crying?

When you are faced with what appears to be an unresolvable problem do you state the problem to the Lord through tears as you are kneeling before him or do you stand up tall and talk it out with him until he leads you to a faith confession?

> **John 11:40-45** Jesus said to her, "Did I not tell you that if you believed, you would see the glory of God?" So they took away the stone. And Jesus looked upward and said, "Father, I thank You for having heard me. I knew that You always hear me, but I have said this for the sake of the crowd standing here, so that they may believe that You sent me." When he had said this, he cried with a loud voice, "Lazarus, come out!" The dead man came out, his hands and feet bound with strips of cloth, and his face wrapped in a cloth. Jesus said to them, "Unbind him, and let him go." Many of the Jews therefore, who had come with Mary and had seen what Jesus did, believed in him.

Why did Jesus raise Lazarus?

a. He wanted to show the Jews that he had great power so that they would believe in him.

b. He loved Lazarus and Martha and Mary.

c. He met the faith confession of Martha with the confirming miracle that she desired.

d. He was teaching his disciples that his power was stronger than death—even four days dead in the tomb.

e. Other?

Why was Jesus willing to remind Martha to believe so that she would see the glory of God in the resurrection of her brother?

Who can we remind of what, so that they can see the glory of God in their life this week?

Burial Customs

Death and everything associated with death was undesirable and unhappy for the Hebrews, beginning with Abraham's tears for Sarah. When the Law was given to Moses, much of it pertained to death. Both sides of death were regulated—for the deceased and the survivors. A proper burial was a sign of respect for the dead, even for one's enemy. When denied, as in the injustice toward the sons of Rizpah and Saul, and his five grandsons, Rizpah took up the cause of the deceased and drove off bird and beast for five months before generating enough sympathy that King David heard and rescinded his orders, granting a proper burial for the seven wronged men (2Samuel 21:8-14).

Becoming Unclean

Included in the regulations related to the dead were who was to die, when, how, and why. Also a main theme was the treatment of the dead body and everything it touched. Specifically, anyone who touched the dead body of any human being was unclean for seven days. The seven day rule held for death by natural causes, war, accident, or punishment. In addition, the actual dead body did not have to be touched, just touching a human bone or grave enacted the seven day rule. Also a person could become unclean for seven days without touching, but just being there when or coming into the place where someone died ((Numbers 19:11, 14, 16).

The Cost of Staying Unclean

When a person who had touched a dead body

did not complete the purification ritual, she or he was unclean and defiled the LORD's tabernacle or sanctuary. In addition the individual who did not become purified would be cut off from the assembly and Israel (Numbers 19:13, 19). Along the same lines, Hebrew law said the land would be defiled if a crucified criminal was not taken down after his death and buried that same day (Deuteronomy 21:23).

Becoming Clean

In order to be clean a person was required by the Law to be purified with water on the third and seventh days. Failing to do so meant that a person remained unclean and cut off from Israel because water "was not dashed on" her or him. In addition, the unclean person was to take some of the ashes of the burnt purification offering, along with running water in a vessel, and make a mixture to be sprinkled.

Then a clean person was to dip hyssop in the mixture and sprinkle the mixture on the deceased, those in the presence of the deceased, on the tent where the person died, and on all of the furnishings in the presence of the deceased. This was to be done on the third and seventh days of the uncleanness. In the same way, the ash mixture was to be sprinkled, via the hyssop, upon whoever touched a human bone, a slain person, a human corpse, or the grave of a human being (Numbers 19:12-13, 17-19).

Even the clean person who sprinkled the unclean on the third and seventh day had to wash their clothes and bathe themselves in water in order for themselves to be clean at evening time. If touched, even the water used for cleansing would make someone unclean until evening. To carry the contamination one step farther, everything the unclean person touched became unclean and would contaminate anyone who touched what the unclean person had touched—the toucher being unclean until evening (Numbers 19:19-22).

Treatment of the Dead

The Hebrew Law contained specific instructions for how to treat the body of the dead. For example, those who were crucified were not to hang all night after they died. They were to be buried the day they died (Deuteronomy 21:23). It is widely held that the Hebrews buried their dead the day they died, if at all possible. One practical reason is because of the immediate decay brought on by the heat of that region. One example which may confirm the rapid decay theory is found in the raising of Lazarus from the dead after four days, when Martha reminds Jesus that there is already a "stench" (John 11:39).

Preparation of the Body

It was unusual that Jacob's body was embalmed. Embalming was done by the Egyptians—a forty day process. Jacob was then brought back to the family tomb in Canaan (Geneses 50:2). Joseph was also embalmed, but placed in a coffin and left in Egypt until his bones were taken back to Canaan at the time of the Exodus (Gen. 50:13, 26).

For the most part, little was done to the body of the deceased. It was washed and then it was wrapped. If available, aromatic herbs, spices, or perfumes were used to anoint or sprinkle upon the body and between the layers of white linen strips.

By the time of Jesus, it was a practice that spices

were used to anoint the body of the deceased. Some mixtures of burial spices included myrrh and aloes. The spices may have weighed more than a hundred pounds. Strips of cloth were used as wrapping, binding the hands and feet tightly to the body, much like a mummy. However, it is believed that the face was wrapped differently, with a cloth that could be removed like a napkin (Mark 16:1; Luke 24:1; John 11:44; 19:39).

For the burial of Jesus, because his death took place late in the day right before the sabbath observance, time did not allow for the customary rituals of preparing the body. But Joseph [of Arimathea] and Nicodemus did manage to remove Jesus from the cross and wrap his body, using a hundred pounds of myrrh and aloes, sprinkling the mixture between the layers of clean white linen strips (John 19:39). The scriptures tell us that Mary Magdalene and the other Mary watched this process. Apparently there was more that should have been done because they came at first light with more spices and ointments to give Jesus a proper burial the morning after the sabbath (Mark 16:1; Luke 23:56; 24:1). The custom was that the dead person's body was washed by family and friends, as was described when Tabitha, also known as Dorcas, died (Acts 9:37) Then the body was anointed with scented oils. The wrapping of the body began at the hands and feet, layering the strips with the spices.

Burial Locations

The first three sets of Hebrew Matriarchs and Patriarchs were buried in a cave off a field (Gen. 23:19; 25:9; 49:31; 50:13). The nurse of the second Hebrew Matriarch was buried under an oak tree (Gen. 35:8).

The second Hebrew Patriarch buried his second wife in a grave by the side of the road, setting up a pillar of remembrance for her (Gen. 35:19-20). A man who was punished by being stoned by all of Israel was buried under "a great heap of stones" (Joshua 7:26).

Ezekiel 32:27 describes the burial of warriors who died in battle. These men appear to have been left where they had fallen on the battlefield. Their swords were placed under their heads and their shields were placed over their bones. Others were buried without details (1 Samuel 31:12).

From their contact with the Greeks, the Jews adopted some of the more elaborate, eclectic architecture and built large mausoleums among the burial caves and tombs of their ancestors.

In the time of Jesus the burial cave or sepulcher was a place which had been cut out of a soft rock and generally only affordable to the fortunate families. With places for one or more bodies to lay "with their fathers" in the family tomb, the decomposition took place until only bones remained. Then the bones were moved to another smaller alcove within the tomb. The tomb's entrance was also its exit and would have a stone that would be rolled in place as a door to keep out scavengers—man and beast. The tombs were outside of the city, but never to the west of Jerusalem because that was the direction of the prevailing winds. When Jesus went to raise Lazarus from the dead, he found him lying in a tomb that was a cave with a stone laying against it (John 11:38). The stone must have been large and heavy because it took more than one person to remove it (John 11:41).

For less fortunate families, their dead were buried in graves. Others were buried by covering the body with stones and soil. For those too poor to buy a plot of ground, special places were set aside for group burials. Foreigners without burial arrangements could be interned in a place such as the potter's field which was bought with the thirty pieces of silver returned by Judas upon his failed plan for Jesus to seize power upon his betrayal (Matthew 27:7).

Funeral Practices

A funeral procession from the point of death to the internment location generally took place with the whole town in attendance. Perhaps it did not begin that way, but as the procession made its way through the streets, anyone who saw or heard it was morally, if not legally, compelled to joint the mourning group.

Families who could afford it hired "mourning women" who were skilled at lamenting. The mourning women were known for their ability to incite everyone present to tears over the deceased. Helping with the mourning process, Jeremiah 9:17-18 describes the skills of women mourners who are quickly able to raise a dirge that makes everyone cry. Amos 5:16 further depicts the "skilled in lamentation" as being called to mourn and wail in the streets. The ritualistic lamentation of weeping and wailing also included the raising of arms in unison, chanting, and giving specific gestures associated with grief. Hired mourners knew just what to do when and how to make a funeral a success.

Jesus encountered a funeral in progress when he passed through the town of Nain. When he saw the mourners wailing he was filled with compassion and raised the only son of a widow, after he told her not to weep (Luke 7:11-15). When Jesus showed up four days after the death and funeral of Lazarus, there was still much weeping, as the tradition called for one week of mourning. When Jesus wept, the crowd equated the tears of Jesus to a demonstration of how much Jesus loved Lazarus (John 11:35-36).

Mourning Practices

For Jacob, who died in Egypt when his son Joseph was a high ranking official, they spent seventy days in mourning weeping for Jacob in Egypt and weeping another seven days after they arrived at his burial site, before interning him (Gen. 50:3). At the death of Israel's first High Priest Aaron and also for Moses, the congregation mourned thirty days for each (Numbers 20:29; Deuteronomy 34:8). Even a captive slave woman was allowed a full month to mourn the death of her immediate family member before she could be taken as a wife (Deuteronomy 21:11-13).

Weeping, lamenting, and mourning sometimes was accompanied by laying on the ground, fasting, refusing perfume and oil to anoint the mourner, and either tearing of clothes or wearing punishing (sackcloth) clothes (2Samuel 1:11-12; 13:31; 14:2; Joel 1:8). King David sang his lamentation over the death of his friend Jonathan and King Saul, who had been his enemy (2Samuel 1:17-27). Others lamented in song, also, throughout the ages (Chronicles 35:25). However, lamenting for the dead was not to include cutting or tattooing the flesh of the mourner or shaving certain parts of the hair (Leviticus 19:28; Deuteronomy 14:1).

To sum it up, death and mourning were not just personal activities, but included family, friends and even the community. People who did not know the deceased were included in the mourning process, and sometimes even hired or compelled to participate. The parting of death was the unhappiest of life's events.

Messiah

In theology, Messiah means the Anointed One. Messiah was and is the Hebrew name for the deliverer of the world, as promised by God. Christ is the Greek equivalent of the Hebrew word Messiah.

Messiah as Expected

The concept of the Messiah as a person with a combination of attributes includes the priestly tradition, the king from the linage of King David, and the suffering servant, as well as the following:

• Personal and national "Deliverer" (2Samuel 22:2; Psalms 18:2; 40:17; 70:5; 140:7; 144:2).

• The "branch" of David's linage (Isaiah 11:1; Jeremiah 33:14-16; Zechariah 3:8; 6:12; Isaiah 4:2).

• Immanuel, "God with us" (Isaiah 7:14).

• "Wonderful Counselor, Mighty God, Everlasting Father, Prince of Peace" reigning on David's throne (Isaiah 9:6-7).

• The servant suffering for his people (Isaiah 53).

• "Mighty Conqueror" (Isaiah 63:1-6).

• The Lord coming to his temple (Malachi 3:1).

Messiah as Revealed

From Mary's conception of Jesus by the Holy Spirit, the fulfillment of Jesus as God's promised Messiah was announced or acknowledged in at least the following instances:

• An angel appeared to Joseph of Nazareth in a dream and announced Jesus as Messiah from his conception (Matthew 1:21).

- At his birth the angel of the Lord announced Jesus as Messiah to the shepherds (Luke 2:11).

- In the Temple at Jerusalem, Simeon declared before Mary and Joseph of Nazareth that infant Jesus was the Messiah (Luke 2:26).

- In the Temple at Jerusalem, Anna told everyone in the temple that infant Jesus was the Messiah (Luke 2:38).

- During his baptism by John the Baptist, God spoke from heaven declaring Jesus Messiah (Mark 1:11).

- After baptizing Jesus, John the Baptist told Andrew and another of his disciples that Jesus was the Messiah (John 1:36).

- After being with Jesus, Andrew told his brother Simon Peter that he had found the Messiah (John 1:41).

- After a lengthy conversation, Jesus told the Samaritan Woman at the Well that he was the Messiah she was waiting for (John 4:25-26).

- Many from Samaria told the woman who met Jesus at the well that they were also sure that he was Messiah (John 4:42).

- Before a crowd, demons acknowledged Jesus as Messiah (Luke 4:34, 41).

- When discussing the death of Lazarus, Martha confessed to Jesus her belief that Jesus was Messiah (John 11:27).

- After Jesus asked Peter, Peter acknowledged Jesus as Messiah (Matthew 16-16; Mark 8:29; Luke 9:20).

Messiah Fulfilled

Description	Prophecy	Fulfillment
Of woman's seed	Genesis 3:15	Galatians 4:4
Will overcome serpent	Genesis 3:15	Hebrews 2:14-15
From Abraham	Genesis 12:1-3	Galatians 3:16
Star out of Jacob	Numbers 24:17	Luke 3:34
Of tribe of Judah	Genesis 49:10	Hebrews 7:14
Seed of King David	Isaiah 11:1-2,10	Acts 13:22-23
Born in Bethlehem	Micah 5:2	Luke 2:4-7
Called Immanuel	Isaiah 7:14	Matthew 1:22-23
Born of a virgin	Isaiah 7:14	Matthew 1:18-25
Infants killed	Jeremiah 31:15	Matthew 2:16-18
Fled to Egypt	Hosea 11:1	Matthew 2:13-15
Preceded by forerunner	Malachi 3:1	Mark 1:1-8
Galilean ministry	Isaiah 9:1-2	Matthew 4:12-16
Zeal for God's house	Psalm 69:9	John 2:17
Prophet of God	Deut. 18:15-18	Acts 3:20-23
Man of sorrows	Isaiah 53:3	Matthew 8:20
Rejected by his own	Isaiah 53:3	John 1:11
Rejected chief cornerstone	Psalm 118:22	1Peter 2:4,7
Priest after Melchisedec	Psalm 110:4	Hebrews 6:20
Jerusalem entry	Zechariah 9:9	Matthew 21:1-11
Betrayal by a friend	Psalm 41:9	Mark 14:10
Forsaken by disciples	Zechariah 13:7	Matthew 26:31
Sold for 30 silvers	Zechariah 11:12	Matthew 26:15
Silver bought a field	Zechariah 11:13	Matthew 27:6-7
Silent before accusers	Isaiah 53:7	Matthew 26:62-63
Beaten	Isaiah 50:6	Mark 14:65
Hair plucked out	Isaiah 50:6	Mark 14:65
Spit on	Isaiah 50:6	Mark 14:65
Suffered for others	Isaiah 53:4-6	Matthew 8:17
Crucified with sinners	Isaiah 53:12	Matthew 27:38
Pierced hands and feet	Psalm 22:16	John 19:36-37
Mocked	Psalm 22:6-8	Matthew 27:39-44
Insulted	Psalm 22:6-8	Matthew 27:39-44
Given poison and vinegar	Psalm 69:21	John 19:29
Pierced side	Zechariah 12:10	John 19:34
Cast lots/divided clothes	Psalm 22:18	Mark 15:24
Bones not broken	Psalm 34:20	John 19:33
Given rich man's tomb	Isaiah 53:9	Matthew 27:57-60
Raised from the grave	Psalm 16:10	Matthew 28:1-9

Martha of Bethany
Facts, Legends, & Concepts

- Only in this reference to Martha in Luke 10:40 has the Greek word been interpreted by the writers of Greek lexicons (dictionaries) as referring to domestic duties," writes Margaret Wold, author of *Women of Faith and Spirit.* Continuing, she points out that John "views Martha in the role of 'server' (again the same word as the one used for the service of deacons and ministers) at a supper given for Jesus and his disciples (John 12:2)." Wold states that Martha "was assuming a role not given to women in the orthodox Jewish community. Women were not permitted to be present at male gatherings." Martha may have been functioning as a forerunner of deacons (Acts 6).

- An ancient apocryphal gospel records Martha among those who were present at the crucifixion of Christ.

- It is also believed that Martha was among those women who went to the tomb early in the morning in order to anoint the dead body of Jesus with the customary burial spices.

- Legend says that Martha, her sister, and brother were banished from Palestine with other Christians. The unbelievers set them adrift on a raft without a rudder or oars to send them to their death. But instead of perishing at sea, they landed in France and Martha continued to have a fruitful ministry.

- In 1431, Lucas Moser painted "Martha, Lazarus and Maximinus after landing at Marseille", now at the Magdalene Altar at Tiefenbronn. A pictorial story of their journey remains on the altar at Tiefenbronn. After their landing in France the three from Bethany became involved in missionary work, with Lazarus becoming a bishop.

• The Martha tradition says that she went to Rhone and led an ascetic life. Martha become a vegetarian and directed a convent. Her life was devoted to spiritual matters and she preached, healed the sick, and even raised someone from the dead who had wanted to hear her preach.

• An ancient legend says that Martha overcame a dragon named Tarascus, a half-animal and half-fish who was reported to be bigger than an ox and longer than a horse. This dragon had teeth like swords which were pointed like horns. The dragon was symbolic of the old order, evil, and what was demonic. Martha conquered the dragon and saved the people who sought her help.

• Tradition says that Martha met her death by drowning as she swam across a river.

• One of many paintings of Martha from the Middle Ages (1517) showing "Martha Defeating the Dragon" is in Nuremberg at the Church of St. Laurence.

• While Martha came along on the coattails of her brother Lazarus and as a secondary figure to her more popular sister Mary, in the south of France, Martha was the object of veneration for herself alone by the tenth century.

• An the eleventh century church in Tarascon was named for Martha, claiming that her relics were there.

- At the Pilgrimage Church of Madonna d'Ongero in Carona, near Lugano, Martha appears in an early eighteenth century sculpture, with a cross in one hand and held by the other hand, what appears to be a tethered dragon lying subdued at her feet.

- From the twelfth century through the end of the Middle Ages, Martha was taken as the role model and often the name of women's religious and social groups and organizations who were rebelling against the hierarchical orders in church and society.

- Martha was made the patron saint of churches and communities specializing in care for the plague sufferers, such as the Humiliati, the Franciscans, and the Compagnia della Morte.

- An order of monks dedicated to care for victims of the plague built a Martha church above Lugano. It remains in a half-ruined state today. Inside, Martha is pictured in Gothic frescoes as a white clothed guardian nurse, consecrating the kneeling brothers of the order to their service to the suffering.

- Around 1300, a mystic and Dominican monk named Meister Eckhart preached the Martha and Mary story in Luke to contrast the wise, prepared virgin Martha with the pleasure-seeking, self-absorbed woman, Mary.

- In 1336, in a chapel in the Church of Santa Croce in Florence, Giovanni di Milano portrayed Martha as the host at Bethany and illuminated her with an inner light.

- Dominican preachers painted Martha. One was Fra (friar's title) Angelico who painted "The Prayer of

Jesus in the Garden of Gethsemane" in the Monastery of San Marco in Florence. In its foreground are Martha and her sister who are identified by their names in their haloes. They are awake as Peter, James, and John sleep. While the disciples recline, Martha sits erect, with eyes alert and hands steepled in prayer, keeping watch as Jesus prays.

- Dominicans named hospitals and homes for widows after Martha, erecting her statue in them.

- Martha is pictured in Jacob Acker's fifteenth century painting, alongside Mary Magdalene at the Magdalene altar of Tiefenbronn. (For some time Mary Magdalene was incorrectly thought to be Mary of Bethany.)

- Ignatius Loyola, founder of the Jesuit order (in 1534), is reported to have held Martha in special veneration.

- Nuremberg is home of a pilgrim's hospital which had a small mediaeval Martha church associating her as a patron saint concerned with activism.

- Martha has been immortalized through art in a painting by Velazquez, about 1618, "Christ in the House of Martha and Mary" comprised of two scenes—in the kitchen and at the feet of Jesus—based on Luke 10.

- Altdorfer, about 1520, painted Martha as one of the women around the Virgin in "Christ taking leave of his Mother."

- Martha is a central character in DeVos' 1625 painting of "The Raising of Lazarus."

Reflection

Martha's siblings were Mary and Lazarus. They lived in the town of Bethany, just two miles from Jerusalem. Each sibling is remarkably distinct from the others. For example, Lazarus is silent and inactive in the Gospels. However he is loved by Jesus, raised from the dead, and was one among others who ate at the table with Jesus. Also, after his resurrection, Lazarus was the focus of a plot to be killed so that people would stop seeing him as evidence of an immortal soul and spirit. Traditionally, Lazarus, the shortened version of Eleaser, has been identified as the "disciple whom Jesus loved" and as the anonymous author of the Gospel we now attribute to John. While the assertions for the authorship of Lazarus are based on scripture references (John 11:3; 21:20-24; Acts 4:13), tradition prefers to credit John with the unique Gospel. For example, John's Gospel does not include the birth of Jesus, parables of Jesus, Sermon on the Mount, lepers or demons. Neither are the twelve disciples listed by name, nor are bread and wine at the last supper. Instead, are the inclusion of lengthy discourses, unlike the short, pithy sayings of the Synoptic Gospels (Matthew, Mark, and Luke). The tradition of the Orthodox church believes that Lazarus left Israel and became a bishop. The legend says that he was the Bishop of Marseille, but Marseille is now believed to be incorrect. However, without controversy, Lazarus was revered by the early church, Palm Sunday eve being his feast day.

Mary is discussed in detail in Chapter Seven, Mary of Bethany, in this book. Traditionally, Martha has been viewed as being overly concerned with the needs of everyday life or domestic details. When compared to her sister Mary, Martha has been judged negatively as the earthly minded sister. Contrariwise, Mary has been seen in a more positive light, as the spiritual sister concerned with things that are Heavenly or Divine. For more information on this and other facets of this comparative concept, please consult *All the Women in the Bible: Sisters & Sisterhood,* Chapter Five, Martha & Mary.

Undeniably, Martha was a woman of action. Upon our first introduction to her in the scriptures she is demonstrating awareness of her many tasks and assertively asks for the help of Jesus to get her sister's assistance to complete them in a timely and appropriate manner. What Martha does not know is that Jesus has come into her home and into her life to reprioritize the needs of her heart.

In one brief interchange with Jesus, Martha learned to chose between being worried and distracted or the better part, which would not be taken away from her (Luke 10:41b-42). When we see her again in serving mode six days before Jesus' last Passover, we see Martha serving without complaint while Mary anoints Jesus. But serving without complaint was not the focus of what Jesus wanted to teach Martha.

When we examine her encounter with Jesus after the death of her brother Lazarus, we can see that Martha learned the most important lesson Jesus had for her. In this scenario Martha is a role model for us today. Let us take a closer look at what she did.

First, after the death of Lazarus, Martha got up and went out to meet Jesus. She sought him. When we are comfortably nestled at home in the comfort of who or whatever consoles us, we have two choices. We can remain where we are physically, emotionally, and spiritually or we can do what Martha did when she: stood up, stood out, and stood with Jesus. First, Martha stood up when she heard Jesus was coming and felt the prompting to go to him. Second, she stood out from the current mind-set of the mourners and went to meet Jesus, instead of staying inside of herself and her problem. Finally, instead of staying and weeping over the situation with the empathizing mourners, Martha stood in the presence of Jesus.

But all of the steps it took for her to get to Jesus were just the beginning of the process. Then Martha talked with Jesus. She stood face to face with him and poured out her heart and soul. When we are talking with Jesus we have two choices. We can tell him what is bothering us and then go away or we can do what Martha did: stay in his presence, state the case, and secure the solution. Instead of weeping at his feet, Martha stood facing Jesus with composure, confidence, and courageousness. Next, instead of just telling him what was bothering her and going away, Martha continued to dialogue with Jesus until she knew the solution to her problem. Then, instead of concluding the interaction when she knew she had made her request to Jesus in faith, she continued to remain in the presence of Jesus and dialogue with him even longer, until she had faith enough to believe for the solution to appear.

Then Martha acted on what she believed. She did what was necessary to bring about the solution she wanted. When we are believing God through faith in Jesus for our miracle, we have two choices. We can continue to expect the impossible to happen or we can do what Martha did to make it happen: confess Jesus as the Christ, stand in the midst of the problem situation with Jesus, and agree with Jesus to open the door, or roll away the stone, for the miracle to walk through. Instead of playing it safe and protecting herself, Martha confessed to Jesus that she believed that he was "the Messiah, the Son of God, the one coming into the world" (John 9:22; 11:27), even though it had become dangerous to say so openly before the Jews. Next, instead of hiding from the reality of the problem, Martha stood with Jesus facing the tomb of her brother. Then, instead of wanting the miracle to appear without effort, Martha gave the sign to roll back the stone door of the tomb and let the stench come out with her resurrected brother.

Most people think the miracle story ends there, but Martha did something else. When her miracle was standing in its wrapping at the door of the tomb, Martha brought it back into her life. When our miracle appears we have two choices. We can chalk one up for our side and go on about our business or we can do what Martha did: unwrap it, bring it home, and show it off. Instead of letting Lazarus remain bound by his grave-clothes after Jesus did his part, Martha and/or her helpers did their part and unbound Lazarus and let him go. Then, instead of leaving Lazarus at the door of the tomb where the miracle appeared, Martha did her part in bringing Lazarus home to what was probably first called Martha's house and would now be called the house of Lazarus—both where Martha served (Luke 10:38-42; John 12:1-3). Lastly, instead of enjoying her miracle privately, Martha did her part and showed off her resurrected brother at the dinner parties she served.

So, Martha demonstrated qualities of character which allowed her to maintain her virtue of service, but also move beyond her traditional feminine role and be the first person to experience resurrection. One explanation for Martha's assertive role in Lazarus' resurrection may be explained by Elisabeth Moltmann-Wendel, author of *The Women Around Jesus,* who portrays Martha as a strong woman, " the rebel, who does not toe the line." In a somewhat softer tone, Joyce Hollyday, author of *Clothed with the Sun,* views Martha as a "servant activist." Rudolf Bultmann writes in his book on *The Gospel of John,* by the same title, that Martha's faith is stronger than Mary's.

In many ways, Martha is a role model for every woman who cannot escape her domestic responsibilities, a role model for every woman who needs as little as help and as much as a miracle, and a role model of communication and relationship with the Divine.

But this story and the other accounts that include Martha are not included in the scriptures so that we would know her and appreciate her virtues. The story is really about what Jesus did for Martha. A wise and understanding reader will value Martha's story as a model of what Jesus can and wants to do for the reader.

When we see Martha interact with Jesus, we see the humanity of Jesus meeting the humanity of Martha. When we see Jesus interact with Martha, we see the Divinity of Jesus drawing out the spirituality of Martha. When we see Martha and Jesus interact on the same level of the acknowledged power of the Divine we see resurrection for Lazarus.

As Martha and her questions were welcomed and answered by Jesus, we can come assertively into the presence of the Divine and dialogue. No matter how desperate we are, no matter how hurt we have been, no matter how long we have suffered, and no matter how impossible it looks, a miracle is possible. Jesus said he was the door (John 10:9, KJV). We must give the orders to roll away our unbelief stone in order for our miracle to walk out, showing the glory of God.

Martha of Bethany

Luke 10:38, 40-41; John 11:1, 5, 19-21, 24, 30, 39;12:2

Martha of Bethany invited Jesus into her home. Jesus became the friend of Martha, regardless of or because of Jesus correcting Martha's attitude about the importance of spiritual matters versus domestic matters. Martha entertained Jesus and his disciples on many occasions, serving them meals as well as hospitality. When her brother became very ill, Martha and her sister sent for Jesus. Jesus delayed and Lazarus died. When Martha confronted Jesus as a friend, he was direct with her also—and Lazarus was raised from the dead.

Focus Virtue: Friendliness

One who forgives an affront fosters friendship, but one who dwells on disputes will alienate a friend.

Proverbs 17:9

Martha displayed her friendliness by inviting Jesus into her home. In her eagerness to show her friendliness through her domestic skills, Martha could have heard an affront in the words of Jesus, *"Martha, Martha, you are worried and distracted by many things; there is need of only one thing. Mary has chosen the better part, which will not be taken away from her"* (Luke 10:42). But the friendly act of taking an interest in another person allowed Martha to receive the words of Jesus. When we are friendly to someone, we hear things differently and we say things differently—with warmth and concern.

Friendliness will be in my heart to be interested,
in my mind to be courteous, on my face to show warmth,
on my lips to say kindness,
and in my hands to do good things.

Virtues Reflection:
Martha of Bethany

Martha of Bethany is a practical example of the possibilities of using our virtues. Admittedly, she had the need to develop some of her virtues, as well as demonstrate some of her developed virtues. But she demonstrated some developed virtues quite well. Martha is a character in three scenarios in the Gospels. In each of the three scripture passages Martha is an active participant. Her action in the first encounter gained her a rebuke, but she learned. In the same way, we can learn from our encounters and rebukes.

Before answering the following questions, read all scripture references relating to Martha and her encounters with Jesus. While you read, reflect, and discuss the story of Martha, think about which virtues you can identify in her. *(You may want to review the Focus Virtues list in Chapter One.)*

1. What are the developed, under-used, and undeveloped virtues you identify in Martha?

2. Which one of the developed virtues of Martha do you most appreciate, today? Why this virtue?

3. What do you admire most about Martha and/or her Focus Virtue: Friendliness?

4. How has Friendliness been part of your life in the past or in the present?

5. How do you see Friendliness or the need for it in your life, now?

6. What can you do to further develop Friendliness in your life?

7. What has helped you most as a result of this study relating to Martha?

Action Scripture

Hebrews 12:28-13:2 *Therefore, since we are receiving a kingdom that cannot be shaken, let us give thanks, by which we offer to God an acceptable worship with reverence and awe; for indeed our God is a consuming fire. Let mutual love continue. Do not neglect to show hospitality to strangers, for by doing that some have entertained angels without knowing it.*

Grateful Prayer

Miraculous God, You are the giver of all good gifts. We thank you for the small miracles of how you suspend this planet in space, supply everyone with enough air to breathe, and bring a seed to harvest. We thank you for the big miracles of faith, hope, and love. We thank you for the gigantic miracles of salvation, resurrection, and eternal life. I thank you for showing me your goodness towards me by seeing the immortality of my soul and spirit, as You demonstrated for Martha through the resurrection of her beloved brother. Let us see Your power working in our lives and in the lives of those we care about. Help us come into your presence and stay there until our faith is miracle faith. Then help us take our miracle faith back into situations that You are ready to resurrect to the glory of God. When we see Your miraculous power at work, show us how to praise and glorify God, properly. We humbly ask all this in the name of Jesus, AMEN.

In the Next Chapter...

you will read and discuss the scripture passages related to the encounter between the Hemorrhaging Woman and Jesus. Understanding the Hemorrhaging Woman means understanding her perception of her situation. To help, the sections that follow in the chapter address the concepts of The Garment of Jesus, Facts About Hemorrhaging, and How to Get What You Say! The Reflection discusses the restoration of Jesus for all who are ailing. A brief summary about the Hemorrhaging Woman and her Focus Virtue: Gentleness are next, with the Virtues Reflection and discussion questions following. The chapter concludes with an Action Scripture and a Grateful Prayer.

Chapter Five

Hemorrhaging Woman

*A woman with faith in God through Jesus Christ is
a woman on a collision course with a miracle.*

Christine M. Carpenter

> Mark 5:25-26 Now there was a woman who had been suffering from hemorrhages for twelve years. She had endured much under many physicians, and had spent all that she had; and she was no better, but rather grew worse.

What do you think the Hemorrhaging Woman had to endure under many physicians?

a. She had to apply stinky, sticky ointments on a potice to her affected area—this was suppose to scare the blood back into her body.

b. She had to drink bitter potions whenever she felt her flow—they would attracted the blood inside her body and keep it there.

c. She had to eat a diet void of any meat because it contained blood—the supposed cause of her trouble was brought on and sustained by her eating foods containing blood, thus keeping, too much blood in her system that her body had to rid itself of.

d. She was cut on various places on her body—then the blood she was hemorrhaging would change its course and come to the cut where the physician was suppose to be able to stop it by creating a scab on the cut.

e. Other?

What have you endured under physicians?

What was the final result of your treatments?

> Luke 8:44a She came up behind him and touched the fringe of his clothes.
> Mark 5:27-28 She had heard about Jesus, and came up behind him in the crowd and touched his cloak, for she said, "If I but touch his clothes, I will be made well."

What had she heard about Jesus?

a. He was a healer of women.

b. He touched unclean people and things.

c. He healed all who came to him.

d. Touching even his clothes made people well.

e. Other?

Why did she come up behind Jesus?

a. She did not want to bother him.

b. If it did not work, she would not be on the spot.

c. He was hurrying away and she could not get in front of him to ask his help, face-to-face.

d. She was hiding because she was "unclean" and it was illegal for her to be in a crowd or to touch anyone.

e. Other?

Why does the scripture tell us that she "said" she would be well if she could touch his clothes?

a. That is what the Gospel writer heard her tell Jesus.

b. It was a common practice to touch something of someone's to get their power or magic.

c. Jesus only healed people who said they believed he would.

d. The writer wants people to say what they want.

e. Other?

Mark 5:29 Immediately her hemorrhage stopped; and she felt in her body that she was healed of her disease.

How did she know she was healed immediately?

a. She stopped feeling the stream flow from her.

b. She felt her body close where it had been open for the flow.

c. She had a "knowing" that she was healed.

d. She felt well again.

e. Other?

Why did she receive her healing immediately?

a. She had waited for twelve years and it was her time.

b. She believed she would be healed.

c. Her faith was high enough to reach God.

d. She went to the right person, at the right time, for the right thing, and said the right words.

e. Other?

Have you ever been healed immediately of any kind of physical problem or symptom?

What?

When?

Where?

How?

> Mark 5:30 Immediately aware that power had gone forth from him, Jesus turned about in the crowd and said, "Who touched my clothes?"
> Luke 8:45a Then Jesus asked, "Who touched me?"

What do you think could have been the sign to Jesus that power had gone forth from him?

a. He became light headed.

b. He was drained and could not walk on.

c. He felt an electrical charge go out of his body.

d. His spirit felt a surge of Divine power flow through him.

e. Other?

Why does Mark write "my clothes" and Luke "me"?

a. Jesus said both things and each writer heard the opposite one, only.

b. Touching clothes is the same as touching the person.

c. Both writers said the same thing but the translators used different words.

d. The writers chose different words to get the idea across to their specific audience.

e. Other?

What does it mean to you when you read that "Jesus turned about in the crowd . . ."?

[Luke 8:45b When all denied it, Peter said, "Master, the crowds surround you and press in on you."] Mark 5:31 And his disciples said to him, "You see the crowd pressing in on you; how can you say, 'Who touched me?' "
Luke 8:46 But Jesus said, "Someone touched me; for I noticed that power had gone out from me."

Why did Peter point out to Jesus that the crowds surrounded and pressed in on him?

a. Peter was a physically oriented man observing the obvious of the moment.

b. Peter was defending the people in the crowd.

c. Since everyone denied touching Jesus, Peter wanted to get away from the crowd and go on to the ruler's house where they were to heal a young girl.

d. Peter did not understand what Jesus meant by power going out of Jesus and did not think the crowd understood either, so he tried to get Jesus to drop the subject before it hurt Jesus' image.

e. Other?

Can you recall any details about a time when you experienced power going out of you?

Can you recall any details about a time when you experienced power coming into you?

> Mark 5:32-34 He looked all around to see who had done it. [Luke 8:47 When the woman saw that she could not remain hidden, she came trembling; and falling down before him, she declared in the presence of all the people why she had touched him, and how she had been immediately healed.] But the woman, knowing what had happened to her, came in fear and trembling, fell down before him, and told him the whole truth. He said to her, "Daughter, your faith has made you well; go in peace, and be healed of your disease."

Why would Jesus not go on before finding the person who had touched him?

a. He wanted an explanation.

b. He wanted to hear how the person tapped into his power without his permission.

c. He wanted to know what happened to the person as a result of tapping into his power.

d. He wanted to validate the faith of the person who touched him.

e. Other?

In parting, why did Jesus tell the woman that: 1) her faith made her well, 2) to go in peace, and 3) to be healed of her disease?

a. He wanted her to believe for and get other things.

b. He wanted her to be sure she knew she was healed by his words and her faith, as much as her words and his power.

c. He was always teaching the crowd and used her.

d. He was reviewing what they talked about.

e. Other?

The Garment of Jesus

The scriptures say that the Hemorrhaging Woman touched either the hem or fringe of Jesus' clothes. According to *Strong's Exhaustive Concordance of the Bible,* the Greek word used in the text to identify hem or fringe may be translated to mean either fringe or tassel. The word translated into clothes or cloak may be translated from the Greek into apparel, cloke [cloak] clothes, garment, raiment, robe, or vesture.

In Numbers 15:37-40, the LORD said to Moses:

Speak to the Israelites, and tell them to make fringes on the corners of their garments throughout their generations and to put a blue cord on the fringe at each corner. You have the fringe so that, when you see it, you will remember all the commandments of the LORD and do them, and not follow the lust of your own heart and your own eyes. So you shall remember and do all my commandments, and you shall be holy to your God.

What the Hemorrhaging Woman may have touched as Jesus went by could have been fringe or a tassel on his prayer shawl. The prayer shawl, called a tallit, has tassels on its four corners. The Israelite tradition was to wear the prayer shawl to express reverence. Deuteronomy 22:12 says, *You shall make tassels on the four corners of the cloak with which you cover yourself.* It has been suggested that the covering of the head of the praying man with his prayer shawl made a secret chamber (Matthew 6:6) in which he could privately, quietly, and humbly gain audience with God in prayer.

Facts About Hemorrhaging

A hemorrhage is the excessive discharge of blood. Hemorrhaging is caused by a pathological condition of the blood vessels or by a traumatic rupture of one or more of the vessels. Hemorrhaging can be a symptom of a complication of many diseases.

<u>One Type of Hemorrhage</u>

Hemorrhages can occur in a variety of places and for a variety of reasons. The Hemorrhaging Woman had the type of hemorrhage that was a chronic flow of blood after the menstrual type of flow. It must not have been a rarity, because the law dealt with the regulation of just such cases (Leviticus 15:19-33).

<u>Cause and Treatment of Hemorrhage</u>

Even during the time of the ministry of Jesus, very little was know about the causes and cures of bodily malfunctions. Generally, only the symptom was treated, and often by superstitious methods combining products of nature with incantations, prayers, and magical rites. While Rome had trained physicians and hospitals to mainly treat its troops, outlying areas such as Palestine had few trained physicians.

The Talmud provided a variety of remedies for the kind of hemorrhage from which the woman with the issue suffered. The Talmud is a two-part collection of Jewish civil and religious writings, the Mishnah being comprised of the text and the Gemara comprising the commentary. While its traditions were not written down until about 220 AD, they were most likely developed by Jesus' day. One of its recipes for a hemorrhage cure consisted of a tonic of rubber, alum, garden crocuses, and wine. The sufferer was to drink the dissolved potion. Eating Persian onions that had been cooked in wine was another remedy. In addition to ingested remedies, the Talmud prescribed the wearing of a linen bag around the neck for months. The bag was to contain the ash of the egg of an ostrich. Another cure administered externally required the patient to rub herself with salves made from foul-smelling concoctions.

Law Governing Those With Hemorrhage

Leviticus 15:19-33 When a woman has a discharge of blood that is her regular discharge from her body, she shall be in her impurity for seven days, and whoever touches her shall be unclean until the evening. Everything upon which she lies during her impurity shall be unclean; everything also upon which she sits shall be unclean. Whoever touches her bed shall wash his clothes, and bathe in water, and be unclean until the evening. Whoever touches anything upon which she sits shall wash his clothes, and bathe in water, and be unclean until the evening; whether it is the bed or anything upon which she sits, when he touches it he shall be unclean until the evening. If any man lies with her, and her impurity falls on him, he shall be unclean seven days; and every bed on which he lies shall be unclean. If a woman has a discharge of blood for many days, not at the time of her impurity, or if she has a discharge beyond the time of her impurity, all the days of the discharge she shall continue in uncleanness; as in the days of her impurity, she shall be unclean. Every bed on which she lies during all the days of her discharge shall be treated as the bed of her impurity; and everything on which she sits shall be unclean, as in the uncleanness of her impurity. Whoever touches these things shall be unclean, and shall wash his clothes, and bathe in water, and be unclean until the evening. If she is cleansed of her discharge, she shall count seven days, and after that she shall be clean. On the eighth day she shall take two turtledoves or two pigeons and bring them to the priest to the entrance of the tent of meeting. The priest shall offer one for a sin offering and the other for a burnt offering; and the priest shall make atonement on her behalf before the LORD for her unclean discharge. Thus you shall keep the people of Israel separate from their uncleanness, so that they do not die in their uncleanness by defiling my tabernacle that is in their midst. This is the ritual for those who have a discharge... becoming unclean thereby, for her who is in the infirmity of her period...who has a discharge, and for the man who lies with a woman who is unclean.

Effect of Hemorrhaging

One effect of hemorrhaging for twelve years, as the Hemorrhaging Woman did, would be anemia. The Greek word for "bloodlessness" is anemia. Anemia is an abnormal condition brought on by a reduction in the number of red blood cells or in their hemoglobin content. Red blood cells carry oxygen to various parts of the body. Anemia causes varied symptoms in its victims, because their body tissues do not receive an adequate delivery of oxygen. In this case, anemia was the direct result of a continual loss of blood. Therefore, being unable to produce enough blood to replace what she lost, she probably suffered from an iron-deficiency and its affects.

Some symptoms of anemia are pallor, shortness of breath, and low vitality. In addition, anemia may cause digestive disorders, dizziness, and weakness. When there is a disturbance in the circulation of the blood, which may be caused by fatigue, pain, or abnormal blood pressure, fainting may occur.

Treatment of Anemia

In her day, the Hemorrhaging Woman endured many things at the hands of physicians, and only grew worse. Until her miraculous healing through Jesus, she was doomed to suffer daily until she finally succumbed to her disorder. In modern times, the treatments of anemia have included:

- The removal of the spleen or the uterus
- Repeated transfusions of blood
- Vitamins and a diet rich in liver
- Where acute blood loss occurs, transfusions are still used
- Iron-deficiency anemia is often treated with iron tablets
- Pernicious anemia is treated with injections of vitamin B_{12}
- Erythropoietin, a synthetically manufactured product, which is naturally produced by the kidneys, is given to certain anemia sufferers to stimulate the production and growth of red blood cells

How to Get What You Say!

The teaching of Jesus is clear. Just as he helped others learn to receive what they wanted or needed, today we can do the same to both receive for ourselves and help others get what they need or want. Scripture is clear about asking and receiving.

First, Jesus often asked people what they wanted him to do for them (Matt. 20:21, 32; Mark 10:51; Luke 18:41; John 4:27). Second, he often discussed their request with them at length in order to expose their faith. Third, Jesus did what God gave him power to do. Fourth, he commended the receiver for her or his faith in God to get what she or he requested.

In Mark 11:23-24, Jesus said:

> *"Truly I tell you, if you say to this mountain, 'Be taken up and thrown into the sea,' and if you do not doubt in your heart, but believe that what you say will come to pass, it will be done for you. So I tell you, whatever you ask for in prayer, believe that you have received it, and it will be yours."*

But how can we be sure that we believe in our heart what we are asking for with our mouth? Perhaps in this regard this old story will help you as much as it has helped me over the years. As I recall, the story takes place at Niagara Falls where a daredevil is getting ready to cross the Falls on a tightrope. As onlookers began placing bets on his success or failure, the daredevil approaches them. He asks who among the crowd really believes that the daredevil will make it across to the other side safely. After overwhelmingly convincing confirmation from one man in particular, the daredevil again asks, "You are sure I will

145

make it?" "I am $100,000 sure. How much surer could anyone be?" He said, "Then Sir, you will not have any objections to climbing up on my back and letting me carry you across to the other side." The daredevil's final remark to the betting man will forever help all believers know for sure if they truly believe.

But how can we be sure that what we believe in our heart is the right thing and not something destructive or displeasing to God? Psalm 37:4 tells us that if we delight in God, the desires we have in our heart have been placed there by God. Of course, when we agree with God's desires in our heart, God gives them to us! Also, in Psalm 21:2, it is clear that God gives the king [David] his heart's desire as spoken by the "lips." We too are kings and priests of God to whom are granted our heart's desires when spoken by our lips. Psalm 145:19 promises that God will fulfill our desires if we fear and reverence the LORD. In addition, in John 15:7 Jesus said that: *If you abide in me, and my words abide in you, ask for whatever you wish, and it will be done for you.*

Jesus taught that believing happens in the heart (Mark 11:23; Luke 24:25; Rom. 10:10). We believe in and with our spiritual heart, not our mind, intellect, reason, or brain.

Jesus taught that when people do let their heart become slow to receive, grow dull, and become hardened, God will give them exactly what they want (Matt. 13:15; Mark 3:5; 10:5; Luke 24:25; John 12:40; Acts 28:27; Eph. 4:18; Hebr. 3:12). We make the choice, first, and then God gives us what we have chosen to be open or closed.

Jesus taught that we could let in or keep out whatever we wanted to have in our heart (Matt. 13:19-23; Mark 4:15-20, 31-32; Luke 2:19, 51; Eph.

1:18). We decide what to give a home to in our heart when worries, distractions, desires, and disappointments present themselves to us, as well as hope, faith, and trust.

Jesus taught that the Holy Spirit would lead and guide us into all truth (John 16:13; Acts 15:8). We can only be led and guided to the degree we seek and allow our direction and parameters to be revealed to us when in the presence of the Holy Spirit.

Jesus taught that the heart can be strengthened and encouraged (Luke 18:1; 2Cor. 4:1, 16; Eph. 3:13; Col. 3:21; Hebr. 12:3, 5). We may chose to seek strengthening and encouraging thoughts, encounters, and environments or remain in fatiguing and discouraging attitudes, relationships, and situations.

Jesus taught that we have what we believe in our heart which gives energizing power to what we say (Mark 11:23-24; Rom. 10:8-10). We will receive whatever we believe in our heart—*not our head*—when we put our beliefs into words.

Jesus taught that words spoken are spirit and life (John 6:63). We may speak about the problem, the condition, and the trouble and get more of the same, or speak of the solution, the remedy, and the cure and get what we say.

Jesus taught that what comes out of our mouth is only what is in our heart in abundance (Matt. 12:34; 15:18; Mark 7:21; Luke 6:45; John 7:38). We may replace our negative words with positive statements from the scriptures, prayers, praises, and other spiritual input until it is in abundance and positive words spill out of our mouth.

Jesus taught that what comes out of our mouth from our heart will either justify or condemn us (Matt. 12:34-37; 15:18; Luke 19:22; Rom. 3:4; 10:8-

10). We may bless or curse others, things, and situations, but at the same time we are giving an even greater dose of the like to ourselves.

Jesus has given us specific detailed instructions of one way that we can receive what we ask for, so that our joy would be complete. Another reason given for fulfilling our request is so that God would be glorified (John 14:13). Yet, how often do we neglect the proper demonstrations of gratitude to the Divine for receiving what we asked for, finding what we have sought, or having the door opened for us?

Another important reason for receiving what we ask for is so that we may be fruitful disciples of Jesus. Jesus said that he chose us and appointed us to bear the kind of fruit that will last and that is one reason why God will give us anything we ask for in the name of Jesus (John 14:14; 15:16; 16:23). Jesus is trusting us to remain close to him and his teachings so that all things we desire will be in line with what Jesus would want for us and those around us. So, whatever we really believe and ask for when using the name of Jesus is exactly what God would want us to have.

When people request things that God can see will not bring them this wealth or fulfillment he has for them, then God has to use "tough" love and abide by a higher law to protect us from ourselves. The parent-child analogy often works well to explain a love that knows that "no" or "not yet" is the best answer for some requests. Therefore, it is with faith in God's will for us that we can pray for anything our heart desires and only God's best will be given to us.

In short, we are given the requests we make because they: 1) help us bear lasting fruit for God, 2) glorify God, and/or 3) make our joy full. All three are what Jesus came to earth to do—and does still!

Reflection

According to Herbert Lockyer, author of *The Life and Times of All the Women of the Bible,* early church tradition said that the Hemorrhaging Woman whom Jesus healed was Veronica and she lived in Caesarea Philippi [or Berenice of Veronica, according to Edith Deen, author of *All the Women of the Bible.*]. A legend about her says that when Jesus was carrying his cross to Calvary, she used her handkerchief to wipe the blood and sweat from his brow. Afterward, while caressing the cloth with reverence, she discovered the imprinted image of Jesus' face in the bloodstained linen. Veronicas are face cloths or any other garment with the representation of the imprinted features of the face of Jesus.

In addition to the traditions about this woman is a record of the historian Eusebius. Around 320 this Bishop of Caesarea wrote in his *Ecclesiastical History* that he visited Caesarea Philippi, finding physical evidence of this woman. He wrote that with his own eyes he saw at the gate of her house what were two brazen figures. One was a woman bending on one knee, making supplication. The other was a representation of Jesus with outstretched hand, offering to help the supplicating woman. The people of the town told Eusebius that the woman had the figures erected to show her gratitude for her healing. Veronica was Sainted, her day being July 12.

But the most interesting things about the Hemorrhaging Woman are found in the scriptures. First and foremost, she was a woman with enough faith to reach out and take her healing. While the purity law that forbid her to touch anyone was killing her personal, social, family, and religious life, that notable day she chose to live by a higher law of faith. According to Jesus, it was her faith that made the connection to his power, resulting in her healing.

Even more than making a connection for her healing by her faith, this woman received something better. She had approached Jesus as a woman without a kinship or religious community connection. It was not her fault. The law said that everyone and everything she touched became unclean for as little as until evening of that day and as long as a full week. No one could touch her or be touched by her. No one could sit where she had sat, lay where she had laid, or touch what she had touched. If they did, they would not be able to participate in religious or any other community or professional activities and would be treated in the same manner as she—unclean.

The scriptures say that once she had money enough to be able to afford more than one physician. Whatever resources she had were now gone and we find her alone. Without a protector to help her through her daily life, the Hemorrhaging Woman may have become a casualty waiting to succumb. Perhaps she was not at the hem of Jesus to be inconspicuous or because she could not nudge her way through the crowd. Instead, she may have been too weak to get up and was fortunate enough to have positioned herself where he would have to pass by within her reach.

However, when she broke the rules and grabbed for God's healing power, through Jesus, she became connected to the Divine. No longer did she lack a family, because Jesus welcomed her into the new family order he was establishing—comprised of those who do God's will. Now Jesus called her "daughter" in front of the entire crowd.

When this occurred, Jairus, an important leader

in the synagogue, was taking Jesus home to heal his daughter. Jairus heard Jesus pronounce this woman clean. He heard Jesus give her status as his daughter, meaning she was under the protection of Jesus. Now she had kinship and religious connections.

The Hemorrhaging Woman had timidly approached Jesus from behind, just touching the fringe of his garment. If Jesus had not stopped to confront her, she not only would have missed out on hearing him call her daughter and recognizing her faith, but her healing would not have become a living testimony of God's power working through Jesus. But he did stop and she did come forward. As a result, the Gospel of Matthew (14:35-36) says that when people knew Jesus was coming they sent word to the entire region so that everyone who was sick could be brought to Jesus for healing, begging him to let them "touch even the fringe of his cloak". For all who came to Jesus, as the Hemorrhaging Woman, all who touched were healed.

Again, Jesus refused to let traditions and laws create barriers between him and the one in need. He will do the same for us, today. He will not be elusive—he makes himself known. He will not be made unclean—he makes clean. He will not be re-jected—he accepts. He will not be exclusive—he is inclusive. He will not hurry away—he stops and waits. He will not be silent—he speaks up. He will not be interrupted—he has time for everyone. He will not chastise—he praises. He will not forsake us—he will make us his daughter.

Interestingly enough, this woman's story is in the middle of another story in which Jesus is on his way to heal the twelve-year-old daughter of Jairus. At the point that the woman is healed of her twelve-year disability, the news arrives of the death of the twelve-year-old girl. The similarities of the two stories are intriguing. Both females end the life they have lived the past twelve years. Both females are called "daughter." Before contact with Jesus, the woman had grown worse, and Jairus' daughter had grown worse. The hand of both females make contact with Jesus and begin a new life.

The contrasts between the two females are noteworthy, also. Jairus' daughter was linked to an influential religious leader, her father, but the Hemorrhaging Woman was an outcast of her religious and family communities. The woman said what she wanted, in faith through Jesus, but Jairus' daughter said nothing and believed nothing of record. The crowd was allowed to observe Jesus' interaction with the woman, but put outside during Jesus' interaction with the girl.

How much the same are our encounters with Jesus. At the same time, how very different our encounters can be, one from another. The differences in our encounters with Jesus are not just between one person and another, but between our encounter today and the encounter people experienced with Jesus years ago. It is often too easy to forget the time during the depth of our weakness when our faith rose up in a hopeless situation and we reached out and took hold of the Divine—barely, by the fringe—and we received what we had said. Again, today, we can reach, touch, and receive our miracle. Herbert Lockyer, reminds us:

> If a person suffers for a while from a complaint and seeks no medical advice, but in the end goes to the doctor, he invariably says, "You should have come to me sooner." But it is the glory of Christ that He can heal those who come late to Him.

Hemorrhaging Woman
Matthew 9:18-22; Mark 5:21-34; Luke 8:40-48

After twelve years of blood draining weakness, endless laundering, and financial poverty from extensive doctors visits and treatments, the bleeding continued unabated. In addition, the Jewish law decreed her "unclean" (Leviticus 15:25-27)—viewing her as cursed and contagious. Under the law she was not allowed to be in a crowd, which may be why she was down at the hem level when she touched the garment of Jesus as he was hurrying to heal the daughter of an important man. But Jesus stopped for this anonymous outcast. Her touch had not been a yank or tug, but a gentle brushing of a transference between spirits. When Jesus stopped at her touch and confronted the crowd, she came forward and told him all. He returned to her gentleness and called her "daughter," commended her faith and sent her away healed and in peace.

Focus Virtue: Gentleness

Let your gentleness be known to everyone.
The Lord is near.

Philippians 4:5

The religious system of her day boldly demonstrated that women's biology was feared. But Jesus shattered the old law that condemned this woman to an isolated, rejected, and shamed life. Her part was that she was able to keep faith in Jesus in the face of years of infirmity, and when she touched him, he refused to be unclean. Instead, he celebrated her faith. Jesus is the same yesterday, today, and forever—for every woman. When we touch Jesus in faith, Jesus will respond and celebrate our faith by granting us healing and peace, calling us "daughter".

I know that the Lord is near so I am gentle with everyone.

Virtues Reflection:
Hemorrhaging Woman

The Hemorrhaging Woman is an example of the extent to which we can use the virtues we each have within us. Hopefully, we are not as isolated and unsupported as she was when she had to make her way, alone, to get into the presence of Jesus in order to solve her problem. Think about what that must have been like for her.

While you read, reflect, and discuss the story of the Hemorrhaging Woman, think about which virtues you can identify in her. *(You may want to review the Focus Virtues list in Chapter One.)* Spend a few minutes identifying and focusing on her developed virtues and then complete the following exercise with her in mind.

1. Which of the developed virtues of the Hemorrhaging Woman do you most appreciate, today? Why?

2. How has her Focus Virtue: Gentleness been part of your life in the past or in the present?

3. How do you see Gentleness or the need for it in your life, now?

4. What can you do to further develop Gentleness in your life?

5. What has helped you most about this Bible story about the Hemorrhaging Woman, her virtues, or this reflection?

Action Scripture

Mark 11:22-24 *Jesus answered them, "Have faith in God. Truly I tell you, if you say to this mountain, 'Be taken up and thrown into the sea,' and if you do not doubt in your heart, but believe that what you say will come to pass, it will be done for you. So I tell you, whatever you ask for in prayer, believe that you have received it, and it will be yours."*

Grateful Prayer

Might God, You are always ready and able to give us what we ask, in faith. We thank You for what we have received from You already. And now we acknowledge our faith in You, God, and we ask for the mountain that is standing in our way to be taken up and thrown into the sea. Please help us in our unbelief so that we may believe what we say will come to pass, and have it done for us. In this prayer now, we agree in faith that we have received our request and thank You for it now. We praise You for it in Jesus' name, AMEN.

In the Next Chapter…

the interaction between Jesus and the Canaanite/Syro-Phoenician Woman are recorded in the scriptures and examined through the discussion questions. To better understand what took place that day, the History of Canaanite-Phoenicia, as well as Jesus' Miracles Prior to This Request, have been included as sections in the chapter. A verse-by-verse commentary on the encounter of Jesus and the Canaanite/Syro-Phoenician Woman is the focus of the Reflection. The summary of the Canaanite/Syro-Phoenician Woman's interaction with Jesus, and her Focus Virtue: Humility provide examples for today's woman in need of a miracle. The Virtues Reflection and discussion questions allow an opportunity to respond to the use and need for virtues today. An Action Scripture and Grateful Prayer conclude the chapter.

Chapter Six

Canaanite/Syro-Phoenician Woman

The rule of persistence is to try just once more.

Christine M. Carpenter

> Matt. 15:21 Jesus left that place and went away to the district of Tyre and Sidon.
>
> Mark 7:24 From there he set out and went away to the region of Tyre. He entered a house and did not want anyone to know he was there. Yet he could not escape notice.
>
> Matt. 15:22 Just then a Canaanite woman from that region came out and started shouting, "Have mercy on me, Lord, Son of David; my daughter is tormented by a demon."
>
> Mark 7:26 Now the woman was a Gentile, of Syro-Phoenician origin. She begged him to cast the demon out of her daughter.

Where is Tyre?

a. In Egypt.

b. In Assyria.

c. In Phoenicia.

d. In Syria.

e. Other?

Why does Matthew call the same woman a Canaanite when Mark calls her a Gentile of Syro-Phoenician origin?

a. Canaanite refers to her religious affiliation.

b. Syro-Phoenician refers to her nationality.

c. Phoenicia and Canaan occupied the same Mediterranean coastal strip of land in northern Palestine and southern Syria, west of Galilee.

d. All of the above.

e. Other?

Both Matthew and Mark set the scene for the dialogue between the woman and Jesus. What reason do you think Mark had for omitting the shouting of the woman?

Why did the Canaanite woman come out shouting at Jesus?

a. She wanted everyone to hear about her troubles with her daughter so they would understand her difficult situation and have compassion on her.

b. Shouting was the customary greeting in the town she came from.

c. Shouting was the only way she could get his attention, because the disciples would not let her get near Jesus.

d. Her daughter's life depended on getting Jesus to free her daughter of the tormenting demon.

e. Other?

Why did she kneel before Jesus?

a. It was her way of blocking his path so he would have to stop and hear her request.

b. She heard that other people who had knelt before Jesus received their request from him.

c. Kneeling was the customary greeting of a woman to a man.

d. She was humbly presenting herself and her case before Jesus.

e. Other?

> Matt. 15:23 But he did not answer her at all. And his disciples came and urged him, saying, "Send her away, for she keeps shouting after us."
>
> Mark 7:25 but a woman whose little daughter had an unclean spirit immediately heard about him, and she came and bowed down at his feet.
>
> Matt. 15:25a But she came and knelt before him, saying, "Lord, help me."

Why did Jesus appear to ignore the Canaanite woman?

a. He wanted her to depend on her faith before he spoke to her.

b. He knew that shouting indicated desperation, which is lack of belief.

c. He did not want to acknowledge or reward such an expression of a lack of faith.

d. He was testing her determination.

e. Other?

Why does Mark omit the urging of the disciples to send away the woman?

a. Because it was rude of the disciples.

b. Because he would have to mention that Jesus had not responded to the woman when she first started shouting after Jesus.

c. Mark did not want to embarrass the disciples.

d. Mark wanted to get to the real dialogue.

e. Other?

In retrospect, why do you think the Lord waited to answer your prayer?

160

> Matt. 15:24 He answered, "I was sent only to the lost sheep of the house of Israel."
>
> Matt. 15:25 But she came and knelt before him, saying, "Lord, help me."
>
> Matt. 15:26 He answered, "It is not fair to take the children's food and throw it to the dogs."
>
> Mark 7:27 He said to her, "Let the children be fed first, for it is not fair to take the children's food and throw it to the dogs."

Why did Jesus say he "...was sent only to the lost sheep of the house of Israel"?

a. He wanted to see if he could discourage her.

b. He had a limited amount of energy and time, and had to remain focused on ministering to the house of Israel.

c. He wanted to see if the disciples knew who were the lost sheep of the house of Israel.

d. He just wanted to be left alone; that is why he went to Tyre.

e. Other?

After the woman begs him for the sake of her little daughter, why does Jesus delay in granting her request?

a. She was a Gentile.

b. He was really tired and was trying to get re-charged first.

c. He was waiting for her to express her faith in him to heal her daughter.

d. He wanted her to teach the disciples about faith.

e. Other?

> Matt. 15:27 She said, "Yes, Lord, yet even the dogs eat the crumbs that fall from their masters' table."
>
> Mark 7:28 But she answered him, "Sir, even the dogs under the table eat the children's crumbs."

Why does Jesus say that, "It is not fair to take the children's food and throw it to the dogs"?

Where did she come up with such a diplomatic rebuttal?

a. She had been called names before and was well practiced.

b. It was a common saying and reply in that region of the country.

c. She really understood Jesus' mission.

d. She just spoke what was in her heart.

e. Other?

What have you replied in response to rejections given you after you requested something for the good of someone else?

How would you have replied if Jesus said those things to you?

How can we dialogue with the Divine to free our children or other people's children?

> Matt. 15:28 Then Jesus answered her, "Woman, great is your faith! Let it be done for you as you wish." And her daughter was healed instantly.
>
> Mark 7:29 Then he said to her, "For saying that, you may go —the demon has left your daughter."
>
> Mark 7:30 So she went home, found the child lying on the bed, and the demon gone.

How far should we be willing to go to speak up for the needs of a child?

Share about a time when you did speak up for or with a child.

What made Jesus say that her faith was great?

a. Asking for the crumbs demonstrated her faith in just a little bit of Jesus being able to do the job.

b. Her ability to argue with Jesus showed him that she had faith in her cause.

c. She showed Jesus that she would not quit because she believed he would be the person to help her daughter.

d. Shouting, kneeling, and begging were faith acts that backed up her request for crumbs.

e. Other?

If you knew it would happen, what would you ask for the good of others?

History of Canaanite-Phoenicia

Canaan's territory originally stretched west from the Mediterranean Sea to the Jordan River to the east, and north from around Ugarit in Syria or the Euphrates to the brook of Egypt to the south. Phoenicia was the Hebrew translation for Canaan and the narrow strip of land bordered on the west by the Mediterranean Sea and on the east by the Lebanon Mountains, on the north by Arvad and on the south by Tyre. However, over time, Canaan had different meanings, as variously described in the Old Testament (Genesis 15:18; Exodus 23:21; Numbers 13:21, 29; Deuteronomy 1:7; 2Samuel 24:2-8, 15; 1Kings 4:21; 2Kings 4:25; Joshua 13:1, 3).

The Locale

In the time of Jesus, Canaan and Phoenicia shared the same Mediterranean costal strip of land in northern Palestine and southern Syria, west of Galilee. However, when the Hebrews first came to the territory, Canaan occupied the land west of the Jordan River, south of the Dead Sea, later known as Palestine. By the second millennium BC the Hebrews began conquering and occupying Canaanite territory. By King Solomon's reign in the 10th century BC, the Canaanites had been either assimilated by the Hebrews or pushed to a narrow strip of land on the coast of the Mediterranean Sea, north of Samaria.

Sidon may have been the oldest Phoenician city. According to the first century Hebrew historian Josephus, Sidon was founded by Canaan, the grandson of Noah. Canaan was the son of Ham, one of Noah's three sons (Genesis 9:18; 10:6). Sidon was protected on the east by the Lebanon mountain range. The city of Sidon was 20 miles north of Tyre, which Sidon founded later.

The Rule

Recent archeology has discovered that the Canaanites and the Phoenicians were one nation of city-kingdoms prior to the Hebrew conquest of southern Canaan. In time, the Phoenicians developed their own nation to the north. The leading cities were Tyre, Sidon, Byblos (Gebal), and Berytos (Beirut). The two most important ruling Phoenician cities were Tyre and Sidon, alternating rule. The Old Testament calls Phoenicians Sidonians, since Sidon was the first Phoenician city and such an important ruling power.

About 3000 BC the early Neolithic race was replaced by Semitics who came from the east. History shows that invading armies conquered and ruled the territory in succession. Among their conquerors, from the north the Hittites came, from the east the Amorites and Assyrians came, and from the south the Egyptians came. The Egyptian Execration Texts name peoples and princes in Canaan to whom they owe allegiance. About 1800 BC, Egyptian forces withdrew from Canaan. Then King Hiram of Tyre began ruling about 981 BC.

But the easy access of the Phoenicians to the sea and their profitable port resources made the Phoenicians attractive targets for other countries looking for profitable conquests. In time, Phoenicia would be conquered often. The Phoenicians would be incorporated into other empires and subjugated to foreign rulers until there was no more Phoenicia. *Microsoft Encarta Encyclopedia* says that by "AD 64, even the name of Phoenicia disappeared, when the territory was made part of the Roman province of Syria."

The Commerce

As early as 2500 BC Phoenicians may have set sail to Egypt. Phoenicians were great sailors and maintained lucrative maritime trade, possibly to and from as far away as Spain and Brittan. *The Encyclopedia of Bible Life* by Madeleine S. Miller and J. Lane Miller says that as early as 1050 BC Cadiz was founded as an outpost in Spain.

It has been recorded that Tyre was involved in exports that included: Boxwood benches with ivory inlay from Cyprus; oak for oars from Bashan; cedar for masts from Lebanon; linen for sails from Egypt; blue and purple fabric for awnings for the Isles of Elishah; silver, iron, tin, and lead for Tarshish; brass for Greece; emeralds, purple broidered work, linen, and coral for Syria; ivory and ebony for inlay for many islands; wheat, candy, honey, oil, and balm for Judea; wine and white wool for Damascus; riding cloths for Dedan in northwest Arabia; lambs, rams, and goats for Arabia; spices, gold, and precious stones for Sheba and Raamah in Arabia.

The Contributions

Before their complete assimilation, the Phoenicians contributed greatly to civilization, directly through their creativity or indirectly through their imports. Their most important contributions were the alphabet, dying textiles, making glass, and the use of numbers, weights, and measures.

In *A History of Western Society,* John P. McKay, Bennett D. Hill, and John Buckler write that "The

Phoenicians' overwhelming cultural achievement was the development of an alphabet." Their alphabet was unlike any other created before. The Phoenicians assigned one sound to one letter. It was the Greeks who "streamlined" the Phoenician alphabet in the late eighth century BC.

Phoenicia is famous for its Tyrian Purple, a dye. The dye is made from certain mollusks (sea invertebrates) found at Tyre. The purple, bluish red, or crimson dye was used by ancient Romans and Greeks.

Also, Phoenicians are believed to have invented glass. The story goes that one day a ship sailed into the Phoenician harbor at Byblos, located at the mouth of the Belus River. Then the ship was filled with chunks of niter (sodium nitrate). Later, the sailors watched the fire melt out the salt, which then blended with the sand, creating a flow of liquid glass.

Phoenicians found trade easier with the creation, development, and use of numbers, weights, and measures. It is believed that the Phoenician merchant sailors would unload their cargo on a strange beach and write its price in the sand. So it is said our system of numbers evolved from such transactions.

Specifically, the Hebrews are believed to have directly benefitted from the Canaanite-Phoenician culture in many ways. The Hebrew language is believed to have been developed from the Phoenicians. Other contributions to Hebrew culture came in the forms of art, music, and architecture. Even Solomon's Temple reflects Phoenician artistry and architecture.

Phoenician Influence on King Solomon's Temple

Harper's Bible Dictionary says that Solomon's Temple was "built by Phoenician craftsmen from the model of a Phoenician-Canaanite (or Syro-Palestinian) chapel." King Solomon hired King Hiram from Tyre to help build the Temple at Jerusalem. 1 Kings 7:14 says that:

> *He was the son of a widow of the tribe of Naphtali, whose father, a man of Tyre, had been an artisan in bronze; he was full of skill, intelligence, and knowledge in working bronze.*

King Hiram had been a friend of King David, Solomon's father, and Hiram rejoiced to see Solomon build the temple that had been David's desire for the LORD. Solomon offered to pay any amount Hiram asked, and Hiram agreed. For twenty years, every year Hiram was paid in wheat and olive oil. Later he received 20 cities, but he was not pleased with the Galilean cities.

Solomon knew that no one knew how to cut timber like the Sidonians, and Hiram could deliver the best for the temple's ceilings, beams, walls, altar, and doors. So Hiram was to furnish all the cedar and cypress from Lebanon. Hiram's stonemasons were skillful men who hewed large blocks of elegant white limestone for the Temple. Hiram provided Solomon's Temple with gold from Phoenician traders.

In addition, Hiram cast his works in the clay ground of the plain of Jordan, between Succoth and Zarethan. The book of 1 Kings lists the work done by Hiram for King Solomon's Temple, which included: two pillars, two bowls of the capitals on the tops of the pillars, two latticeworks to cover the two bowls of the capitals on the tops of the pillars; the four hundred pomegranates for the two latticeworks, two rows of pomegranates for each latticework, to cover the two bowls of the capitals on the pillars; the ten stands, the ten basins on the stands; the one sea, and the twelve oxen underneath the sea; pots, shovels, and basins. All the vessels made for the house of the LORD were of burnished bronze crafted by King Hiram of Tyre.

Entering the sacred part of the Temple, the nine foot high platform was approached by ten broad steps. On both north and south sides of the steps were twin pillars with lily work, which may have originally been inscribed with the names of other gods, but later were Jachin and Boaz. *The Encyclopedia of Bible Life* by Madeleine S. Miller and J. Lane Miller says that in *Archaeology and the Religion of Israel,* Albright refers to the twin pillars as "a Phoenician model, they were lofty incense stands rightly symbolic with cosmic significance." The authors continue to make the point that such pillars were usually found in sanctuaries in Syria and elsewhere dedicated to the worship of other gods. In defense of Solomon, they add that:

> Solomon naturally might make some concession to the fads of architects in his day. Or his Phoenician builders, having a dydnastic purpose...may have dressed up with Hebrew names, twin pillars which meant something else to them.

Beyond the twin pillars which may have been as high as 30 feet, the steps led through a door, to a vestibule, then to the Holy Place. The 45 feet high, 30 feet wide, and 60 feet long room was lined with cedar and cypress, inlaid with gold leaf. Its furnishings included golden candlesticks, the table of shewbread, and a small altar of cedar inlaid with gold leaf. The room was illuminated by Tyranian-Egyptian influenced clerestory windows rising above the roofs of the flanking aisles.

The final room was the Holy of Holies, about 30 feet square. In it was the Ark of the Covenant, guarded by two 15 foot high cherubim of olivewood and gold. *Harper's Bible Dictionary* says that they "were possibly winged sphinxes of Phoenician origin, or a Phoenician version of Egyptian angel-like deities." Below them, the boxlike Ark of the Covenant contained two stone tablets of the Law, a pot of manna, Aaron's budded rod, and the Presence of Yahweh.

Phoenician influences in other areas of the temple are noted by *Harper's Bible Dictionary*. For example, the altar with four corners and four horns is like that of Canaanite altars. In addition, the cast copper (brass) molten sea, 3 1/2 inches thick, 15 feet in diameter, with its curved up edges, stood on the backs of 12 metal bulls. The bulls were known to be symbolic of fertility and associated with the god Baal.

The collaboration between King Solomon and King Hiram of Tyre, and their craftsmen, may have made Phoenician influences in Solomon's Temple unavoidable and inevitable. Also, over the twenty years of temple building, wise King Solomon let himself stray from the word of the LORD. The LORD had warned him several times, but Solomon persisted with his foreign wives and accommodating their heathen gods. As a result, Solomon became influenced by other gods. 1Kings 11:1-3, 5 says that:

King Solomon loved many foreign women along with the daughter of Pharaoh: Moabite, Ammonite, Edomite, Sidonian, and Hittite women, from the nations concerning which the LORD had said to the Israelites,

"You shall not enter into marriage with them, neither shall they with you; for they will surely incline your heart to follow their gods"; Solomon clung to these in love. Among his wives were seven hundred princesses and three hundred concubines; and his wives turned away his heart. . . .For Solomon followed Astarte the goddess of the Sidonians, and Milcom the abomination of the Ammonites.

Astarte, also known as Ashtoreth and Ashtaroth, was the supreme female deity of the Phoenicians. As a female fertility deity, she was the goddess of love and fruitfulness. Her counterparts in other parts of the world included, Ishtar, Aphrodite, Artemis, and Selene. Found with her altar was often an altar for her male counterpart in worship, Baal. Baal was also associated with Bel since both names mean "owner" or "lord." Baal was important to the Canaanites because of their agricultural society and Baal's control of fertility, particularly the soil and domestic animals.

Microsoft Encarta Encyclopedia says that, "The name *Baal* was compounded with many Hebrew, Chaldean, Phoenician, and Carthaginian personal and place-names, such as Baalbek, Ethbaal, Jezebel, Hasdrubal, and Hannibal." Yet Yahweh continually forbid the worship of other gods (Leviticus 26:30; Psalm 78:58; Numbers 33:52; Deuteronomy 33:29). Even so, in Solomon's Temple in 10th century BC their influences are easily recognizable. It was not until King Hezekiah, in the 7th century BC, that the Temple in Jerusalem was reopened, the foreign idols removed, and the shrines of foreign gods were eliminated completely from Hebrew lands.

Jesus' Miracles *Prior* to This Request

Healing Sickness, Affliction & Disease	*Curing Demoniacs*
Matthew 4:23	
Matthew 4:24	Matthew 4:24
	Mark 1:23-26
	Mark 1:39
Matthew 8:5-13	Matthew 8:28 -33
[Matthew 8:1-3	
Mark 1:40-42]	
[Matthew 8:14-15	
Mark 1:30-31]	
[Matthew 8:16	[Matthew 8:16
Mark 1:32-34]	Mark 1:32-34]
[Matthew 9:2-7	
Mark 2:3-12a]	
	Mark 5:1-15a
[Matthew 9:18 -19	
Mark 5:22-24]	
[Matthew 9:23-25	
Mark 5:35-42]	
[Matthew 9:20-22	
Mark 5:25-34]	
Matthew 9:27b-30a	
Matthew 9:32b-33a	Matthew 9:32b-33a
Matthew 9:35	
[Matthew 12:9-13	
Mark 3:1-5]	
Matthew 12:22	Matthew 12:22
Matthew 14:14	
Matthew 14:35-36	
	[Matthew 15:21-22
	Mark 7:24-26]

Reflection

What would cause the Canaanite/Syro-Phoenician woman to think that Jesus could, or even would, help her daughter? She must have heard that the demons listened to him and came out when he told them to depart. She heard about a man in the synagogue convulsing and crying out with a loud voice when the demon left at the command of Jesus. People said that at Capernaum in just one night many who were possessed were set free of their demons. Jesus had called out the demons from two demonics in the country of the Gadarenes. Another demoniac was mute and when Jesus cast out the demon the mute man spoke. Still another demoniac was both blind and mute, and Jesus freed him of the demon and he could speak and see, also.

She had heard about healings of lepers, the paralyzed, the blind, the deaf, and every other kind of sickness and disease. Jesus healed everyone who asked him. Jesus even raised the dead. He did it for men, for women, and for children.

But she was a Gentile and a foreigner. Jesus had been healing the sick and casting out demons for Jews in the synagogues and streets of their towns. He had left his country to rest. How dare she bother this man with her draining request! But it was for her tormented daughter. She must try for the child's sake.

> *Jesus left that place and went away to the district of Tyre and Sidon. Just then a Canaanite woman from that region came out and started shouting, "Have mercy on me, Lord, Son of David; my daughter is tormented by a demon."*
>
> Matt. 15:21-22

The Canaanite/Syro-Phoenician woman knew Jesus had the power to free her child. Shouting to him was only the first step she was willing to take for her child. Embarrassing? Maybe. But this was her little girl who was being tormented day and night by a demon. Enduring embarrassment was the least she would do to see her child set free.

> *But he did not answer her at all. And his disciples came and urged him, saying, "Send her away, for she keeps shouting after us."*
> Matt. 15:23

Even though he did not answer her, she knew Jesus heard her. At least he did not send her away, like his disciples wanted him to do. Her voice was strong and she was going to persist. She knew she had his attention when Jesus let her continue shouting at him, and explained to his disciples:

> *"I was sent only to the lost sheep of the house of Israel."*
> Matt. 15:24

Jesus must have wondered: Would his disciples understand about the lost sheep of the house of Israel? Would they understand why they were with him in the district of Tyre and Sidon? Would they understand why he did not stop the woman from shouting after them?

> *But she came and knelt before him, saying, "Lord, help me."*
> Matt. 15:25

Finally, by his stopping to tell his disciples that he was sent "only to the lost sheep of the house of Israel" the delay gave her an opportunity to approach Jesus! She did not accuse the disciples of hindering her. She did not reprimand Jesus for ignoring her. She did not stand face-to-face as an equal to a man, a Jew, a Rabbi. Instead, she knelt before Jesus, humbly calling him Lord and making her request.

He answered, "It is not fair to take the children's food and throw it to the dogs."

Matt. 15:26

According to *Eerdmans' Handbook to the Bible,* the term "dogs" was "an abusive term for Gentiles." Jesus wasted no time, but continued to explain the game rules. He was here for the lost, and was only going to feed his own. In other words, Jesus was not going to give a thing to anyone who was not part of his spiritual family.

She said, "Yes, Lord, yet even the dogs eat the crumbs that fall from their masters' table."

Matt. 15:27

This Canaanite/Syro-Phoenician Woman made it clear that she understood and accepted the calling of Jesus to the Jews. In addition, she understood and accepted that he was also master of even the dogs— the Gentiles. Jesus may have deliberately given her the picture in which she could find a way to paint in herself and her daughter.

Then Jesus answered her, "Woman, great is your faith! Let it be done for you as you wish." And her daughter was healed instantly.

Matt. 15:28

How did this mother's faith override the mission of Jesus to the lost sheep of the house of Israel? Jesus talked in puzzles and pictures of similes, analogies, and metaphors. The symbol of sheep is clearly people.

In John 10 Jesus says that his sheep hear his voice and come to him. While many Jews heard the voice of Jesus, they did not follow him—meaning that they were not his sheep. In John 10:14-16 Jesus says:

I am the good shepherd. I know my own and my own know me, just as the Father knows me and I know the Father. And I lay down my life for the sheep. I have other sheep that do not belong to this fold. I must bring them also, and they will listen to my voice. So there will be one flock, one shepherd.

Remember the picture of the one lost sheep being pursued by the shepherd, while the ninety-nine wait for him. It may be that this mother had great faith in Jesus, because she was one of the lost sheep of the house of Israel—of another fold. Jesus may have left the Jews, temporarily, to bring in this Canaanite/Syro-Phoenician mother. Certainly, she did listen to his voice. This woman heard Jesus.

Because she heard the voice of Jesus, Jesus could hear her voice and grant her request. As she was asking to receive something for another person, Jesus was giving her something for that person, and herself. She became the link, the conduit that carried the power from its source, Jesus, to its destination, her daughter.

There were no other recorded healings or signs in Tyre or Sidon at that time. Did Jesus come there just for this Canaanite/Syro-Phoenician woman and her daughter? Were she and her daughter the foundation for the Christian church that would flourish there after the death and resurrection of Jesus? Was the New Testament church a success in Tyre and Sidon as a result of the Canaanite/Syro-Phoenician woman and her demonstration of faith in Jesus? I think so.

Canaanite/Syro-Phoenician Woman
Matthew 15:21-28; Mark 7:24-30

First ignored, then insulted by being equated with a dog, this woman could not be dismissed. She had a daughter who needed to be healed and she knew the healer could say the Word and her daughter would be made well. The disciples did not get it, but Jesus did. Her shouts were declarations of faith. Her persistence got her an audience with Jesus, despite the disciples' aggravation toward her and their well intended protection of Jesus. Even after she persisted until he stopped and talked with her, Jesus dismissed her. But she would not go away. Instead, she humbly knelt before Jesus who continued to talk with her, eventually granting her request—because of her great faith.

Focus Virtue: Humility

The reward for humility and fear of the LORD
is riches and honor and life.

Proverbs 22:4

This Canaanite, also known as the Syro-Phoenician woman, had great faith. But her great faith did her no good until she mingled it with humility. Taking her faith in humility, kneeling at the feet of Jesus, this mother gained life for her daughter and herself. The greatest faith in the world is only obnoxious shouting to those around, even to disciples who walk closely with Jesus, until we bring it to the Lord. And then only when we humbly lay our great faith at the feet of Jesus will we hear his words of healing and deliverance. Like the Canaanite woman, our request made in humility will also be granted in the presence of Jesus. Even a crumb from Jesus is enough to satisfy our greatest need—for ourselves or for others.

My head and my heart will practice humility in the presence of others and in the presence of the LORD.

177

Virtues Reflection:
Canaanite/Syro-Phoenician Woman

Again, we are reminded that the women in the Gospels are able to teach us a variety of things. This woman can teach us about virtues that are to be admired and emulated, such as assertiveness, hopefulness, and determination. Also, she can teach us about our need to exercise our virtues, purposefully. In addition, this mother demonstrates that the need for further development of our virtues is important because what we do or do not do affects our daughters.

Today, when you read about, think on, and discuss the stories of this mother, the Canaanite/Syro-Phoenician woman, identify the developed virtues you see in her. *(You may want to review the Focus Virtues list in Chapter One.)* After reading all the scriptures associated with her, take a few moments to complete the following exercise with her in mind.

1. Which one of the developed virtues of this mother, the Canaanite/Syro-Phoenician woman, do you most appreciate, today? Why?

2. How has her Focus Virtue: Humility been part of your life in the past or in the present?

3. How do you see Humility or the need for it in your life, now?

4. What can you do to further develop Humility in your life?

5. What has been the most valuable part of this study or reflection?

Action Scripture

Matthew 7:7-11 *Ask, and it will be given you; search, and you will find; knock, and the door will be opened for you. For everyone who asks receives, and everyone who searches finds, and for everyone who knocks, the door will be opened. Is there anyone among you who, if your child asks for bread, will give a stone? Or if the child asks for a fish, will give a snake? If you then, who are evil, know how to give good gifts to your children, how much more will your Father in heaven give good things to those who ask him!*

Grateful Prayer

Gracious God, we thank You for giving us good gifts. We ask You for the touch only You can give to us and our loved ones, and we thank You for helping us receive it now. We seek You for things only You can do for us and our loved ones, and we thank You for helping us find what we need. We knock again at the door of our need for us and our loved ones, and we praise You for opening the door. Just as the Canaanite Mother persisted for the sake of her daughter, we persist for the sake of our loved ones. As you blessed her and hers, bless us and ours. Teach us to stop limiting our request to You, standing on our self importance— our ego—but instead to kneel in humility before You and receive Your abundance for us and our loved ones. We pray all this in the name of Jesus Christ our Lord, AMEN.

In the Next Chapter...

the discussion of the scripture passages relating to the encounter between Jesus and Mary of Bethany have a different focus than the same passages discussed in the chapter about Martha. To better understand Mary of Bethany's behavior, the sections that follow in the chapter list the Notable Events During the Last Days in the Life of Jesus, Anointing Facts, and a Comparison of the Women Anointing Jesus. Mary of Bethany Facts, Legends, & Concepts are also included in the chapter. The Reflection tackles the many misconceptions of Mary of Bethany. Then the summary of her encounters with Jesus and her Focus Virtue: Reverence are briefly presented, followed by an opportunity to explore the virtues of Mary of Bethany in the Virtues Reflection. Concluding the chapter are an Action Scripture and a Grateful Prayer.

Chapter Seven

Mary of Bethany

You know your intuition is foolproof
when following your heart leads you to Jesus.

Christine M. Carpenter

> **Luke 10:38-39** Now as they went on their way, he entered a certain village, where a woman named Martha welcomed him into her home. She had a sister named Mary, who sat at the Lord's feet and listened to what he was saying.

Why did Mary sit at the Lord's feet and listen to what he was saying?

a. She heard something he said that interested her.

b. She was curious about Jesus.

c. He had invited her to sit in.

d. She was determined to be included in spiritual matters, even though women were socially and legally excluded.

e. Other?

What do you think Mary heard as she listened to Jesus?

a. She heard how the Kingdom of God was within her.

b. She heard that God loved her and sent Jesus to her and the world.

c. She heard how she could become a minister for God.

d. She heard that she was as valuable to God as the best of men.

e. Other?

When was the last time you listened to the Lord at length?

What was it like?

What happened as a result?

> **Luke 10:40-42** But Martha was distracted by her many tasks; so she came to him and asked, "Lord, do you not care that my sister has left me to do all the work by myself? Tell her then to help me." But the Lord answered her, "Martha, Martha, you are worried and distracted by many things; there is need of only one thing. Mary has chosen the better part, which will not be taken away from her."

What had Mary chosen that was the better part?

a. She chose to listen to Jesus, while Martha chose to direct Jesus.

b. She chose to give her labor to Jesus, while Martha chose to labor for results.

c. She chose to learn about spiritual matters, while Martha chose to postpone spiritual matters.

d. She chose to be in the presence of Jesus, while Martha chose to be in the kitchen.

e. Other?

Why couldn't the better part Mary had chosen be taken away from her?

a. She got it from Jesus.

b. It merged with her heart.

c. She would not let it be taken away.

d. She would always remember it.

e. Other?

When did you have a choice to make between being worried and distracted by many things and choosing the Lord? What happened?

> **Excerpts from John 11:1-6** Now a certain man was ill, Lazarus of Bethany, the village of Mary and her sister Martha....So the sisters sent a message to Jesus, "Lord, he whom you love is ill." But when Jesus heard it, he said, "This illness does not lead to death; rather it is for God's glory, so that the Son of God may be glorified through it." Accordingly, though Jesus loved Martha and her sister and Lazarus, after having heard that Lazarus was ill, he stayed two days longer in the place where he was.

Why was the message sent by Mary and her sister just an announcement that Lazarus was ill?

a. They may have thought that Jesus would come and heal Lazarus when Jesus heard that he was ill.

b. They may have thought that it was understood that the sisters wanted Jesus to come immediately to their home.

c. They may have thought that it would be too much to ask Jesus to change his plans and return to Bethany, but they hoped that he would.

d. Other?

What did Jesus mean when he said, "This illness does not lead to death; rather it is for God's glory, so that the Son of God may be glorified through it."?

What do you think was going through Mary's mind about Jesus as she watched her brother grow worse waiting for Jesus to arrive?

> **John 11:17-20** When Jesus arrived, he found that Lazarus had already been in the tomb four days. Now Bethany was near Jerusalem, some two miles away, and many of the Jews had come to Martha and Mary to console them about their brother. When Martha heard that Jesus was coming, she went and met him, while Mary stayed at home.

How did the Jerusalem Jews console Mary and her sister about their brother?

a. Mary and Martha were given hugs and kisses by the Jews.

b. The Jews cried with Mary and Martha constantly.

c. Mary and Martha were given special mourning foods by the Jews.

d. According to tradition, the Jews were maintaining their seven day mourning ritual by the side of the sisters of the deceased.

e. Other?

Why would the Jews come two miles to Bethany to console two sisters about the death of their brother?

a. Lazarus was an important Jew.

b. Mary was well liked by everyone.

c. Martha was a well known hostess.

d. The Jews heard that Jesus had been called and hoped he would come so that they could see him in person.

e. Other?

When she heard that Jesus was coming, what do you think was going through Mary's mind about Jesus and her brother's death?

> **John 11:28-35** When she had said this, she went back and called her sister Mary, and told her privately, "The Teacher is here and is calling for you." And when she heard it, she got up quickly and went to him. Now Jesus had not yet come to the village, but was still at the place where Martha had met him. The Jews who were with her in the house, consoling her, saw Mary get up quickly and go out. They followed her because they thought that she was going to the tomb to weep there. When Mary came where Jesus was and saw him, she knelt at his feet and said to him, "Lord, if you had been here, my brother would not have died." When Jesus saw her weeping, and the Jews who came with her also weeping, he was greatly disturbed in spirit and deeply moved. He said, "Where have you laid him?" They said to him, "Lord, come and see." Jesus began to weep.

Why did Mary stay at home instead of going with her sister to meet Jesus?

a. She knew Martha would speak for her.

b. She knew she would be called when it was her turn to see Jesus.

c. The sisters had agreed beforehand that Martha would see Jesus alone, first.

d. She was too distraught about the death of her brother to get up and be sociable to anyone, even Jesus.

e. Other?

Why did Jesus wait for Mary at the same place he met her sister?

What do you think Mary should have said to Jesus?

John 12:1-8 Six days before the Passover Jesus came to Bethany, the home of Lazarus, whom he had raised from the dead. There they gave a dinner for him. Martha served, and Lazarus was one of those at the table with him. Mary took a pound of costly perfume made of pure nard, anointed Jesus' feet, and wiped them with her hair. The house was filled with the fragrance of the perfume. But Judas Iscariot, one of his disciples (the one who was about to betray him), said, "Why was this perfume not sold for three hundred denarii and the money given to the poor?" (He said this not because he cared about the poor, but because he was a thief; he kept the common purse and used to steal what was put into it.) Jesus said, "Leave her alone. She bought it so that she might keep it for the day of my burial. You always have the poor with you, but you do not always have me."

Why did Mary anoint Jesus?

a. She wanted to show her gratitude for him for raising Lazarus from the dead.

b. She wanted to make him more comfortable.

c. She was showing loving hospitality.

d. She did not know why she did it, only that her heart compelled her to.

e. Other?

Why did Jesus defend Mary again?

Have you been criticized for showing extravagancy toward Jesus and/or the spiritual? What happened?

Notable Events During the Last Days in the Life of Jesus

Day	Event
Friday	*Feet of Jesus anointed and wiped by the hair of Mary of Bethany at Lazarus' home* (John 12:1-8)
Saturday	
Sunday	Triumphal entry into Jerusalem (Matthew 21:1-11; Mark 11:1-11; Luke 19:28-40)
Monday	Cleansing of the temple in Jerusalem (Matthew 21:12-13; Mark 11:15-19; Luke 19:45-48)
Tuesday	Jesus' authority challenged before the Sanhedrin (Mark 11:27-33; Luke 20:1-8) Jesus foretells his return and the destruction of Jerusalem (Matthew 24:1-2, 15-28; Mark 13:14-27; Luke 19:41-44; 21:20-24) *Unnamed woman anoints the head of Jesus at Simon the leper's house* (Matthew 26:6-13; Mark 14:3-9) Judas bargains to betray Jesus to the Jewish rulers (Matthew 26:14-16; Mark 14:10-11; Luke 22:3-6)
Wednesday	
Thursday	Jesus observes the Passover meal with his disciples and institutes the Memorial Supper (Matthew 26:17-30; Mark 14:22-26; Luke 22:7-19; John 13:1-30) Jesus prays in Gethsemane for himself, for his disciples, and for all believers (Matthew 26:36-44; Mark 14:32-41; Luke 22:39-46; John 17:1-26)

Friday	Jesus is betrayed and arrested in Gethsemane (Matthew 26:47-56; Mark 14:43-50; Luke 22:47-53; John 18:1-12) Jesus is questioned by Annas, former High Priest (John 18:12-14, 19-24) Jesus is condemned by Caiaphas and the Sanhedrin (Matthew 26:57-67; Mark 14:53-65; John 18:24) Peter's denial of Jesus (Matthew 26:69-75; Mark 14:66-72; Luke 22:55-62; John 18:15-18, 25-27) Jesus' formal condemnation by the Sanhedrin (Luke 22:66-71) Suicide of Judas (Matthew 27:3-10) Jesus' trial before Pilate (Matthew 27:1; Mark 15:1-3; Luke 23:1-5; John 18:29-38; 19:1-12) Jesus' appearance before Herod Antipas (Luke 23:6-12) Jesus' formal death sentence by Pilate (Matthew 27:24-26; Mark 15:6-15; Luke 23:13-25; John 19:13-16) *Jesus' crucifixion observed by the women (Matthew 27:55-56; Mark 15:16-41; Luke 23:49; John 19:25-27)* Temple veil torn from top to bottom (Matthew 27:51-56) *Jesus' burial in a new tomb observed by women (Matthew 27:57-61; Mark 15:47; Luke 23:55-56)*
Saturday	Jewish sabbath day of rest
Sunday	*Angel appeared to the women at the empty tomb of Jesus (Matthew 28:2-6; Mark 16:1-6; Luke 24:1-7)* *Jesus' resurrection from the dead declared to women (Matthew 28:1-7; Mark 16:6; Luke 24:1-7)* *Jesus appeared and spoke to women (Matthew 28:8-10; Mark 16:9-11; John 20:11-17)* *Women charged to bring the news of the resurrection (Matthew 28:8-10; Mark 16:7-8; Luke 24:9-12; John 20:18)*

Anointing Facts

The act of anointing is performed by rubbing, smearing, or pouring some substance on or over a person or thing. Anointing dates back to the Egyptians, before the Israelites entered the wilderness. Originally, the act of anointing was a religious ritual. The anointing ritual was reserved for the transfer of holiness and virtue bestowed upon the one being anointed, generally a king or ruler. It was the transfer of a special spiritual endowment from the deity in whose name the rite was being performed.

Since ancient times anointing has been a symbol of the power of God upon the priest or king. The anointing ceremony was the official act of appointing God's man to a specific office. The anointing oil was poured on the head of a priest to consecrate him (Leviticus 8:12). Israel looked for their deliverance from their enemies and the establishment of the presence of God upon the earth as coming from God's anointed one, the Messiah.

Over time, anointing was not confined to the ruling class. Anointing became part of meaningful rituals and ceremonies for ordinary people. The marriage tradition included the anointed bridegroom journeying to get his bride.

Another form of anointing was an act of hospitality. A guest would be anointed upon entering a home, as a way to honor the guest. The anointing mixture was olive oil, often mixed with perfume. It also served as a cleansing agent on exposed parts of the body to lessen the effects of extreme heat and high lime content of the dust around Palestine. Therefore, anointing a guest who had traveled a distance was more than an honor, but also a comfort.

In Matthew 6:16-18 Jesus warned against making a show when fasting. He told the religious men to anoint their head and wash their face. The anointing and washing were probably ordinary practices if their omission was a sign of showing off when they fasted.

Jesus also spoke of the anointing of wounds for healing. In his parable a the good Samaritan has found a man who was attacked and robbed. Among other kindnesses, the good Samaritan anoints the man's wounds (Luke 10:34).

Anointing for burial was also a custom. The body of Jesus was anointed with about a hundred pounds of spices by Nicodemus and Joseph of Arimathea when they quickly placed him in the tomb. The women returned with spices and ointments to the tomb of Jesus the morning after the sabbath in order to properly anoint his body.

Christians are anointed by God. Some Christians are anointed for service and ministry (2Corinthians 1:21). Other Christian anointings teach and abide with the believer (1John 2:27). In addition, anointing can heal the sick (James 5:14).

The "spikenard" Mary of Bethany used to anoint the feet of Jesus was a rare and costly herb/spice. Grown in the Himalayas, camel transports brought spikenard to Palestine. The fragrant oil made from its roots was used to make perfumes and ointments. It has been translated as "perfume" and "nard."

Mary of Bethany's anointing of Jesus has some similarities with another anointing in the Bible. The Shulamite bride tells of her spikenard emitting its fragrance while her king sat at his table (Song of Solomon 1:12). Later, her groom praises her as his sister and spouse with fruits of fragrant spikenard (Song of Solomon 4:13-14).

191

Comparison of the Women Anointing Jesus

Sinner Anointer	Mary of Bethany	Unnamed Woman	Unnamed Woman
[1](last verse in this scripture passage, moved here for clarity) Luke 8:1 [1].*SOON AFTERWARDS* he went on through cities and villages, proclaiming and bringing the good news of the kingdom of God. The twelve were with him...Luke 7:37 And a woman in the	John 12:1 [1]*SIX DAYS BEFORE THE PASS- OVER* Jesus came to	Matt. 26:2 "You know that after [1]*TWO DAYS THE PASSOVER IS* coming, and the Son of Man will be handed over to be crucified." Matt. 26:6 Now while Jesus was at	No [1]. Mark 14:3 While he was at
[2]**city**, who was a sinner, having learned that he was eating in the	[2]**Bethany**, the	[2]**Bethany** in the	[2]**Bethany** in the

³Pharisee's house (see Luke 7:44, Simon), brought an	³home of Lazarus, whom he had raised from the dead. John 12:2 There they gave a dinner for him. Martha served, and Lazarus was one of those at the table with him. John 12:3 Mary took a	³house of Simon the leper, Matt. 26:7 a woman came to him with an	³house of Simon the leper, as he sat at the table, a woman came with an
⁴ALABASTER JAR OF OINTMENT. Luke 7:38	⁴POUND OF COSTLY PERFUME MADE OF PURE NARD,	⁴ALABASTER JAR OF VERY COSTLY OINTMENT, and she	⁴ALABASTER JAR OF VERY COSTLY OINTMENT OF NARD, and she broke open the ⁴JAR and
⁵She stood behind him at his feet, weeping, and began to ⁵*bathe his feet with her tears* (see Luke 7:44-46) and to ⁵*dry them with her hair.*	⁵*anointed Jesus' (feet, and wiped them with her hair.)* The house was filled with the fragrance of the perfume. John 12:4-5 But	⁵*(poured it on his head)* as he sat at the table. Matt. 26:8 But when	⁵*(poured the ointment on his head).* Mark 14:4 But

Comparison of the Women Anointing Jesus continued . . .

Then she continued *kissing his feet and anointing them with the ointment .)* Luke 7:39 Now when

⁶the Pharisee who had invited him saw it, he said to himself,

⁷*"If this man were a prophet, he would have known who and what kind of woman this is who is touching him — that she is a sinner."* Luke 7:40

⁶Judas Iscariot, one of his disciples (the one who was about to betray him), said,

⁷*"Why was this perfume not sold for three hundred denarii and the MONEY GIVEN TO THE POOR?"* John 12:6 (He said this not because he cared about the poor, but because he was a thief; he kept the common purse and used

⁶the disciples saw it, they were *angry* and said,—

⁷*"Why this waste?* Matt. 26:9 *For this ointment could have been sold for a large sum, and the MONEY GIVEN TO THE POOR."* — Matt. 26:10

⁶some were there who said to one another in *anger,* —

⁷*"Why was the ointment wasted in this way?* Mark 14:5 *For this ointment could have been sold for more than three hundred denarii, and the MONEY GIVEN TO THE POOR."* — And they *scolded her.* Mark 14:6

to steal what was put into it.) John 12:7

8Jesus said, "Leave her alone. She bought it so that she might keep it

8But Jesus, aware of this, said to them, "Why do you trouble the woman? 9SHE HAS PERFORMED A GOOD SERVICE FOR ME. Matt. 26:11 For you always have the poor with you, but you will not always have me. Matt. 26:12 By pouring this ointment on my body she has

8But Jesus said, "Let her alone; why do you trouble her? 9SHE HAS PERFORMED A GOOD SERVICE FOR ME. Mark 14:7 For you always have the poor with you, and you can show kindness to them whenever you wish; but you will not always have me. Mark 14:8 She has done what she could; she has anointed my body beforehand

8Jesus spoke up and said to him, "Simon, I have something to say to you." "Teacher," he replied, "Speak." Luke 7:41 "A certain creditor had two debtors; one owed five hundred denarii, and the other fifty. Luke 7:42 When they could not pay, he canceled the debts for both of them. Now which of them will love him more?" Luke 7:43 Simon answered, "I suppose the one for whom he canceled the

Comparison of the Women Anointing Jesus continued . . .

greater debt." And Jesus said to him, "You have judged rightly." Luke 7:44 Then turning toward the woman, he said to [3]Simon, "Do you see this woman? I entered your house; you gave me no water for my feet, but she has [5]*bathed my feet with her tears and dried them with her hair*. Luke 7:45 You gave me no kiss, but from the time I came in she has [5]*not stopped kissing my feet* .Luke 7:46 You did not anoint my head with oil, but [5]*she has anointed my feet with ointment.*

Luke	John	Matthew	Mark
Luke 7:47 Therefore, I tell you, her sins, which were many, have been forgiven; hence she has [9]SHOWN GREAT LOVE. But the one to whom little is forgiven, loves little." Luke 7:48 Then he said to her, [10]**"Your sins are forgiven."** Luke 7:49 But those who were at the table with him began to say among themselves, "Who is this who even forgives sins?" Luke 7:50 And he said to the woman, **"Your faith has saved you; go in peace."** Luke 8:1, see [1] .	[9]FOR THE DAY OF MY BURIAL. John 12:8 [10]**You always have the poor with you, but you do not always have me.**	[9]PREPARED ME FOR BURIAL. Matt. 26:13 [10]Truly I tell you, wherever this good news is proclaimed in the whole world, *what she has done will be told in remembrance of her.*	[9]FOR ITS BURIAL. Mark 14:9 [10]Truly I tell you, wherever the good news is proclaimed in the whole world, *what she has done will be told in remembrance of her.*

Mary of Bethany
Facts, Legends, & Concepts

• Mary is doing the unprecedented: she sits at the feet of a teacher, a rabbi, in the company of men, and receives his teaching and religious instruction..." writes Janice Nunnally-Cox, author of *Fore-Mothers: Women of the Bible.* She adds, "Mary's actions were a distinct break with Jewish custom. Jesus must have encouraged her . . ."

• Margaret Wold, author of *Women of Faith and Spirit,* writes that "Mary was not only affirmed and supported in her action; she was lifted up as a model for women in the years to come." Wold says that "The rediscovery of Jesus' pledge to Mary has been an enormous encouragement to women who have longed to be part of a community of scholars dedicated to the study of God and God's revelation."

• Paul Tillich writes in a chapter called "Our Ultimate Concern" in his book entitled, *The New Being,* that "Mary is concerned about one thing, which is infinite, ultimate, lasting."

• Jesus inspires Mary of Bethany to break out of the cage of conventions and realize that a woman can be something other than a homebody," writes William E. Phipps, in *Assertive Biblical Women.* Phipps continues saying that, "he [Jesus] admires her eagerness for learning and, in effect, her desire to be liberated from the limitations of her gender-defined role."

- Peter Ketter writes in *Christ and Womankind* that "Every housewife should follow Mary's example and for a while free herself to be open to new spiritual impulses."

- On the other hand, Meister Eckhart, author of *Ewige Geburt* writes that "We suspect that dear Mary sits there more out of pleasure than for her spiritual advancement." Eckhart says, "That is why Martha says, 'Lord, make her get up!', because she is afraid that Mary might continue in this delight and not advance in any way."

- Rudolf Bultmann, author of the book entitled, *The Gospel of John,* writes that "In Mary, then, we find a portrayal of the first stage of faith, beyond which her sister had advanced . . . Mary does not have Martha's certainty."

- Elisabeth Moltmann-Wendel writes in *The Women Around Jesus* that (Referring to the frequent but inaccurate confusion between Mary of Bethany and Mary of Magdala.):

> Mary of Bethany suffers the fate of many women: her voice is not loud, what she says is not original, her story is not dramatic. Her behavior is not noticeable, her conduct is modest. She seems sympathetic, but by the next time people have forgotten her name and confuse her with another woman who has made more of an impression.

- Edith Deen, author of *All of the Women of the Bible,* writes that "Mary was following the custom of this time, that of refreshing guests at banquets by pouring cool and fragrant ointments on their heads and sometimes their feet."

- "The Word of God, faith and deeds belonged together, inseparably. Mary felt this in the depths of her soul. She felt a stirring desire to do something," Glin Karssen writes, in *Her Name Is Woman.* "She wanted to express her thankfulness to her Lord, perhaps for the last time . . . Her decision was made," Karssen continues, "The perfume was very costly. The amount in the jar represented a laborer's wages for an entire year... It was time to do something for him now."

- Mary of Bethany was one of three women who anointed Jesus. The first woman to anoint Jesus is unnamed, and referred to as a sinner in Luke 7:36-50. The time of her anointing was early in the ministry of Jesus, probably prior to the death of John the Baptist. In addition, the anointing took place in the city, at the house of Simon the Pharisee (Luke 7:37, 40). While she also bathed the feet of Jesus with her tears and dried them with her hair, her act was one of extraordinary love. After Jesus taught Simon and the crowd a lesson in love and forgiveness, the unnamed sinner was commended and sent on her way.

- The other unnamed woman who anointed Jesus, did it two days before his final Passover. Her act of anointing had a history dating back to Egyptian days before the Israelites entered the wilderness.

Originally, anointing was a religious ritual reserved for the transfer of "holiness and virtue of the deity in whose name the rite was performed, as well as a special spiritual endowment" upon the king or priest, according to *The Family Bible Encyclopedia.* Unlike the unnamed sinner who anointed Jesus early in his ministry and Mary of Bethany who anointed Jesus six days before his last Passover, this woman did not anoint the feet of Jesus, but his head.

- "...her [Mary of Bethany] unusual role was to take her place beside her sister [Martha] in the preparation and serving of food (otherwise her sister would not have complained that Mary had 'left' her to serve alone)..." justifies Margaret Wold, author of *Women of Faith and Spirit.*

- Mary of Bethany was incorrectly thought to be Mary Magdalene when the fifteenth century painter, Jacob Acker, portrayed her alongside Martha of Bethany at the Magdalene altar of Tiefenbronn.

- Many artists have painted Mary of Bethany at the feet of Jesus, listening to him, including: Pieter Aertsz, Constantin Hansen, William Blake, and Jacopo Tintoretto.

- "A Committed Follower" is *The Woman's Study Bible* subtitle for a short biography about Mary of Bethany. Further, the commentary says that "Mary's example demonstrates her strong decision-making capability," referring to her sitting at the feet of Jesus and listening to him.

- Herbert Lockyer writes in *The Life and Times of All the Women of the Bible,* that Mary of Bethany was a "spiritual scholar" sitting at the feet of Jesus listening to his teachings, as did students of the masters, rabbis, or teachers who sat on chairs high above their pupils who were seated on the ground as they listened and learned.

- In *What Paul Really Said About Women: An Apostle's Liberating Views on Equality in Marriage, Leadership, and Love,* John Temple Bristow writes that the Luke 10:38-42 story of Mary of Bethany is an "example of how Jesus welcomed women among his disciples (learners)."

- "Mary is represented as a follower of Jesus who is well acquainted with Jesus' ultimate destiny (compare Judas, the disciple in John 12:4, who is not as well informed)," according to the *Holman Bible Dictionary.*

- *Great People of the Bible and How They Lived* says that Mary of BEthany was showing her devotion toward Jesus by "sitting at his feet, listening to his teaching" for hours at a time.

- Charles Wesley wrote of Mary of Bethany, lamenting:

> Oh, that I could forever sit,
> Like Mary, at the Master's feet:
>   Be this my happy choice:
> My only care, delight and bliss,
> My joy, my Heaven on earth be this,
>   To hear the Bridegroom's voice.

Reflection

Incorrectly, Mary of Bethany has traditionally been a woman of multiple personalities and identifying names. In particular, the majority of her identity problem comes from a composite of the real Mary of Bethany, Mary Magdalene, and the unnamed anointing sinner woman in Luke 7:36-50—with a little Caught Adulteress from John 8:2-11 thrown in for added confusion, along with a hint of the unnamed woman who anointed the head of Jesus two days before his final Passover.

Part of the problem comes from the omission of the particular seven demons cast from Mary Magdalene by Jesus (Luke 8:1-3). Imaginations conjured up the idea of the seven deadly sins, each represented by a demon. More focused imaginations found seven sexual categories of sin to attach as Mary Magdalene's seven demons. One of those sexual categories was adultery, which caused a woman to be brought into the audience of Jesus one mourning at the Temple in Jerusalem. Some think the Caught Adulteress was brought alone because she had turned to prostitution and the scribes and Pharisees who set her before Jesus without her partner were merely presenting a known prostitute who had been caught at some time before but not at that very hour.

When Mary Magdalene's demons were categorized into sins, the next step was easy. It was only reasonable to assume that Mary Magdalene as a forgiven Caught Adulteress, now a delivered sinner, would be grateful to Jesus. Then, out of gratitude for her escape from the stoning planned by the scribes and Pharisees, as well as her freedom from the seven sinful, sexual demons, Mary Magdalene could be identified as the grateful sinner woman who anointed Jesus at the house of Simon the Pharisee, early in his ministry.

Going another step farther, Mary Magdalene, having been set free and forgiven of her past sexual indiscretions, she was free to return to her home and family—a forgiven woman. The brother and sister who had learned forgiveness from their close friend Jesus, of course, welcomed Mary Magdalene back home. So complete was her forgiveness that Martha and Lazarus never spoke of it again, nor did anyone else. In the deal, Mary Magdalene was allowed to keep the name from her "fallen" state as well as her original identification with her hometown of Bethany.

To complicate matters, when Mary of Bethany anointed Jesus just six days before his last Passover, she became identified with the sinner woman who anointed him early in his ministry. Both women anointed the feet of Jesus. A third woman anointed his head just two days before his last Passover. Too often it was easier to merge three anointers into one character. The (dis)similarities between the three anointings of Jesus are laid out side-by-side on the *Comparison of Women Anointing Jesus* table in this chapter. Study will show that three different women on three separate occasions anointed Jesus.

Is it reasonable to think that, naturally, everyone who spoke of her or heard her story knew that Mary of Magdala, known as the Magdalene, was an inter-changeable name with Mary of Bethany—both being the same person? In addition, is it reasonable to think that everyone also knew that she was the sinner woman who anointed the feet of Jesus early in his ministry and the Caught Adulteress and the unnamed woman who anointed the head of Jesus two days prior to his last Passover—all five characters? If so, she was even more well known than Peter, the most prominent of the male disciples of Jesus. Peter, who had formerly been called Simon before knowing Jesus, is identified in all four Gospels by both his former and latter names, often along with a complete explanation of why he had two names (Matthew 4:18; 10:2; 16:16; Mark 3:16; Luke 5:8; 6:14; John 1:42; 6:68; 13:6, 9, 24, 36; 18:10, 15, 25; 20:2, 6; 21:2, 3, 7, 11, 15, 17; Acts 10:5, 18, 32; 11:13). However, are we to believe that such explanations are not necessary for the well known Mary...whoever...whatever?

Truth in fact is that the anointing sinner, the Caught Adulteress, the unnamed anointer, Mary of Magdala, and Mary of Bethany are five different women. The fragments of their stories cannot be overlaid into one person. Such a synthesis occurred only after several centuries had elapsed since the writing of the Gospels. It was a convenient way to distill the points of a sermon. By adding each woman's small ingredient, a concentrated concoction was made that was more potent when served over the pulpit. Unfortunately, then as now, literary license or liberty with the facts were not great concerns when weighed against the motivation to make a point that would accomplish a goal. Therefore, centuries have elapsed but the misconception continues to be perpetuated by and to the lazier student of the Bible.

So, what do we really know about Mary of Bethany? The scriptures give us only three brief glimpses of her. First, she is found silent at the feet of Jesus, listening to him—for which Jesus defends her. Second, she is found mourning for her brother Lazarus, but this time she goes to the feet of Jesus speaking her only biblical line of dialogue, and Jesus does the listening—followed by the resurrection of her brother. Third, she is found silent at the feet of Jesus, anointing and wiping his feet—for which Jesus defends her.

She is seen as the Bible woman who spent the most time at the feet of Jesus. Mary of Bethany has been called the best and the worst among the women in the Bible, depending on the caller's value system. She has been called the most reverent woman in the scriptures. She has been called a learner, a contemplative, and an introspective. On the other hand, she has been called lazy, inconsiderate, and shallow. She has been called the most useless woman in the scriptures, never learning how to put her faith into service for others, thus called the most selfish of woman.

With every positive assertion there is a negative counterpart. Also, every asset becomes a liability when taken to the extreme. Strengths become weaknesses when overextended. Mary's desire to sit and listen to Jesus and Martha's drive to complete her tasks are both strengths—and weaknesses. The correct balance gets things done right—living life to its fullest.

Obviously, Jesus would not have returned to her home if he was never served food or beverage. He did not come to sit and talk and go away even hungrier than when he arrived. After traveling and ministering Jesus needed to replenish himself physically with a good meal. He also need to replenish himself socially and emotionally. Therefore, Jesus would not have returned if Mary of Bethany had not made him feel welcomed, appreciated, and helpful. She was attentive, interested, and absorbed. Jesus knew that he was contributing to her and that she appreciated it and would welcome him back again. Just as Mary of Bethany did, may we all give our guests the physical and spiritual food and replenishing they need.

Mary of Bethany

Luke 10:39-42; John 11:1-2, 19-20, 28, 31-31, 45; 12:3

Mary of Bethany sat at the feet of Jesus, listening to him as her sister prepared for the guests. When Mary was criticized for not helping, Jesus defended her desire to be present in spiritual matters. The week before the crucifixion of Jesus, Mary anointed the feet of Jesus with costly perfume, and wiped them with her hair. When Judas criticized her for the financial waste, Jesus defended Mary for anointing him in preparation for his burial.

Focus Virtue: Reverence

Therefore, since we are receiving a kingdom that cannot be shaken, let us give thanks, by which we offer to God an acceptable worship with reverence and awe.

Hebrews 12:28

Mary: sat at the feet of Jesus, listening attentively and reverently; knelt at the feet of Jesus, submitting respectfully and reverently; wiped the feet of Jesus, serving tenderly and reverently. The deep respect and special care that Mary showed for Jesus is reverence. We can show reverence for the things in our material world as well as for the things in our spiritual world. Reverence is an attitude as well as a practice. Listening, reflecting, and praying during times of stillness can be the beginning of reverence. We can help others develop reverence by our attitude of deep respect for what is sacred to us, to others, and to God.

Everyday I will take time to value the sacred and experience reverence.

Virtues Reflection:
Mary of Bethany

As you read the stories in the Gospels about Mary of Bethany, you may come away with more questions than answers. For several reasons there is a lack of information regarding the motivations behind her encounters with Jesus. Therefore, you may want to dig more deeply into the probable thoughts, emotions, actions, and reactions of Mary. This is important, because as we relate to her we can gain a fuller understanding of what her encounter with Jesus was really like and how it can be a positive role model for us. However, the full impact of her actions may not unfold until we ponder and explore our own questions relating to her encounter, as they remind us of our own circumstances. Before answering the following questions, read all scripture references relating to Mary of Bethany. Then, identify the developed virtues you see in her. *(You may want to review the Focus Virtues list in Chapter One.)*

1. Which developed virtues do you identify in Mary?

2. Which one of Mary of Bethany's developed virtues do you most appreciate, today? Why this virtue?

3. What do you admire most about Mary of Bethany and/or her Focus Virtue: Reverence?

4. How has Reverence been part of your life in the past or in the present?

5. How do you see Reverence or the need for it in your life, now?

6. What can you do to further develop Reverence in your life?

7. What has helped you most as a result of this study relating to Mary of Bethany or her virtues?

Action Scripture

2Timothy 2:15 *Do your best to present yourself to God as one approved by [God], a worker who has no need to be ashamed, rightly explaining the word of truth.*

2Timothy 3:16-17 *All scripture is inspired by God and is useful for teaching, for reproof, for correction, and for training in righteousness, so that everyone who belongs to God may be proficient, equipped for every good work.*

Grateful Prayer

Holy God, we worship You. Our hearts are full of love for You. We pause now in reverence of this moment, in Your presence. Thank you for Your Holy Spirit who leads and guides us into all truth, as we learn as Mary of Bethany did, the teachings of Jesus. We thank You for the scriptures and their ability to give us teaching, reproof, correction and above all, training in righteousness. We ask that You give us strength and every other grace we need to become equipped and proficient in every good work You call us to do. With grateful hearts, reverently we give You praise in the name of Jesus, AMEN.

In the Next Chapter...

you will read and discuss all the scripture passages relating to Mary Magdalene. To help locate the sites of specific events in which Mary Magdalene is a central character, a map of the Jerusalem Area in the Time of Jesus is included in the chapter. A Background of Calvary, the Crucifixion, and Resurrection help provide a context for the events. The Reflection contrasts leader experiences of Mary Magdalene and Peter. The summary of her encounters with Jesus and her Focus Virtue: Steadfastness demonstrate a higher level of spirituality available today. The chapter concludes with the Virtues Reflection and discussion questions, followed by an Action Scripture and Grateful Prayer.

Chapter Eight

Mary Magdalene

*Even when we are misunderstood, we can have
confidence that Jesus understands.*

Christine M. Carpenter

> Luke 8:1-3 Soon afterwards he went on through cities and villages, proclaiming and bringing the good news of the kingdom of God. The twelve were with him, as well as some women who had been cured of evil spirits and infirmities: Mary, called Magdalene, from whom seven demons had gone out, and Joanna, the wife of Herod's steward Chuza, and Susanna, and many others, who provided for them out of their resources.

Why are 1) "some women" and 2) a few women by name, mentioned specifically, as being with Jesus and the twelve—instead of lumping both groups in with the "many others"?

a. They were the females who were Jesus' female apostles.

b, They were the women who witnessed his crucifixion, death, and resurrection at the empty tomb.

c. They were well know women in the Christian community and could verify the author's narrative.

d. They were the sources providing the information written by Luke.

e. The named women were the only women of the 1) some women with the twelve group who were alive at the time of Luke's writing of his Gospel.

f. Other?

Have you or has anyone you have known had a "miraculous" cure, and if so, what happened?

Of what had Jesus cured Mary Magdalene?

Of what specific kinds or types did Jesus effect cures, healings, and deliverances in women, and for whom:

1) Evil spirits?

2) Infirmities?

3) Demons?

Who are the "them" who were provided for out of the resources of the women who were traveling with Jesus and the twelve?

Have you ever or do you now support an individual, individuals, or a ministry able to change lives for the better through the power of God?

How do you provide support and how do they minister?

Matthew 27:55 Many women were also there, looking on from a distance; they had followed Jesus from Galilee and had provided for him. Among them were Mary Magdalene, and Mary the mother of James and Joseph, and the mother of the sons of Zebedee.

Mark 15:40-41 There were also women looking on from a distance; among them were Mary Magdalene, and Mary the mother of James the younger and of Joses, and Salome. These used to follow him and provided for him when he was in Galilee; and there were many other women who had come up with him to Jerusalem.

Luke 23:27-31, 48-49 A great number of the people followed him, and among them were women who were beating their breasts and wailing for him. But Jesus turned to them and said, "Daughters of Jerusalem, do not weep for me, but weep for yourselves and for your children. For the days are surely coming when they will say, 'Blessed are the barren, and the wombs that never bore, and the breasts that never nursed.' Then they will begin to say to the mountains, 'Fall on us'; and to the hills, 'Cover us.' For if they do this when the wood is green, what will happen when it is dry?" . . . And when all the crowds who had gathered there for this spectacle saw what had taken place, they returned home, beating their breasts. But all his acquaintances, including the women who had followed him from Galilee, stood at a distance, watching these things.

John 19:25 And that is what the soldiers did. Meanwhile, standing near the cross of Jesus were his mother, and his mother's sister, Mary the wife of Clopas, and Mary Magdalene.

Why are the specific names of women followers of Jesus mentioned, but no men mentioned by name at the crucifixion?

a. The women who were mentioned were the inner circle of Jesus' female apostles.

b. The women mentioned by name had become well-known in the early Christian community and gave credibility to the story of the crucifixion and resurrection of Jesus.

c. The women named were the only followers of Jesus who were standing close enough to hear what was spoken during the crucifixion and able to testify as sources of Luke.

d. The author was making a point that the male disciples and apostles had abandoned Jesus in his hour of need, but that the women held fast in the face of fear and brutality.

e. Other?

At the crucifixion, what was Mary Magdalene doing in the company of Jesus' family?

a. She knew them well and was considered part of their extended family.

b. It was coincidence that they were all standing together.

c. She was Jesus' most trusted follower and his family clung to her for support.

d. They were all standing as close as they could get to the cross of Jesus.

e. Other?

Why did the women stand near the cross of Jesus?

a. They were curious and wanted to see and hear everything that happened.

b. They were saying encouraging and loving things to him.

c. They wanted him to know they would not forsake him, the way Peter and the others had.

d. They were waiting for requests or instructions he might want them to carry out.

e. Other?

Matthew 27:57-62 When it was evening, there came a rich man from Arimathea, named Joseph, who was also a disciple of Jesus. He went to Pilate and asked for the body of Jesus; then Pilate ordered it to be given to him. So Joseph [of Arimathea] took the body and wrapped it in a clean linen cloth and laid it in his own new tomb, which he had hewn in the rock. He then rolled a great stone to the door of the tomb and went away. Mary Magdalene and the other Mary were there, sitting opposite the tomb.

Mark 15:42-43, 46-47 When evening had come, and since it was the day of Preparation, that is, the day before the sabbath, Joseph of Arimathea, a respected member of the council, who was also himself waiting expectantly for the kingdom of God, went boldly to Pilate and asked for the body of Jesus. . . . Then Joseph [of Arimathea] bought a linen cloth, and taking down the body, wrapped it in the linen cloth, and laid it in a tomb that had been hewn out of the rock. He then rolled a stone against the door of the tomb. Mary Magdalene and Mary the mother of Joses saw where the body was laid.

Luke 23:50-56 Now there was a good and righteous man named Joseph [of Arimathea], who, though a member of the council, had not agreed to their plan and action. He came from the Jewish town of Arimathea, and he was waiting expectantly for the kingdom of God. This man went to Pilate and asked for the body of Jesus. Then he took it down, wrapped it in a linen cloth, and laid it in a rock-hewn tomb where no one had ever been laid. It was the day of Preparation, and the sabbath was beginning. The women who had come with him from Galilee followed, and they saw the tomb and how his body was laid. Then they returned, and prepared spices and ointments. On the sabbath they rested according to the commandment.

John 19:39-42 Nicodemus, who had at first come to Jesus by night, also came, bringing a mixture of myrrh and aloes, weighing about a hundred pounds. They took the body of Jesus and wrapped it with the spices in linen cloths, according to the burial custom of the Jews. Now there was a garden in the place where he was crucified, and in the garden there was a new tomb in which no one had ever been laid. And so, because it was the Jewish day of Preparation, and the tomb was nearby, they laid Jesus there.

Why did Mary Magdalene and the other Mary stay with the dead body of Jesus until it was entombed?

a. The women loved him so much they wanted to be with Jesus for as long as they could.

b. The women believed in the resurrection of Jesus and wanted to be present when he returned to life.

c. The women were responsible for the proper burial of the dead and were observing what needed to be done to complete the process.

d. Other?

Why didn't the twelve apostles help Joseph of Arimathea and Nicodemus with the burial of Jesus?

a. They were afraid for their lives.

b. They knew the women would assist in the burial.

c. They were too distraught, grieving.

d. Other?

Why did the women prepare spices and ointments for the body of Jesus even after they saw about a hundred pounds being used at his internment?

a. They knew it was not enough for a proper burial.

b. They wanted Jesus to have even more perfumes and lovely fragrances than normally given.

c. They wanted a reason to ask for the tomb to be opened so that they could be with Jesus even for a little while in his death.

d. They were mourning by preparing the spices and talking about their beloved Jesus.

e. Other?

Why is Mary Magdalene the person most often recorded as present at the cross, burial, and resurrection of Jesus?

Matthew 28:1-8 After the sabbath, as the first day of the week was dawning, Mary Magdalene and the other Mary went to see the tomb. And suddenly there was a great earthquake; for an angel of the Lord, descending from heaven, came and rolled back the stone and sat on it. His appearance was like lightning, and his clothing white as snow. For fear of him the guards shook and became like dead men. But the angel said to the women, "Do not be afraid; I know that you are looking for Jesus who was crucified. He is not here; for he has been raised, as he said. Come, see the place where he lay. Then go quickly and tell his disciples, 'He has been raised from the dead, and indeed he is going ahead of you to Galilee; there you will see him.' This is my message for you." So they left the tomb quickly with fear and great joy, and ran to tell his disciples.

Mark 16:1-8 When the sabbath was over, Mary Magdalene, and Mary the mother of James, and Salome bought spices, so that they might go and anoint him. And very early on the first day of the week, when the sun had risen, they went to the tomb. They had been saying to one another, "Who will roll away the stone for us from the entrance to the tomb?" When they looked up, they saw that the stone, which was very large, had already been rolled back. As they entered the tomb, they saw a young man, dressed in a white robe, sitting on the right side; and they were alarmed. But he said to them, "Do not be alarmed; you are looking for Jesus of Nazareth, who was crucified. He has been raised; he is not here. Look, there is the place they laid him. But go, tell his disciples and Peter that he is going ahead of you to Galilee; there you will see him, just as he told you." So they went out and fled from the tomb, for terror and amazement had seized them; and they said nothing to anyone, for they were afraid. THE SHORTER ENDING OF MARK [[And all that had been commanded them they told briefly to those around Peter. And afterward Jesus himself sent out through them, from east to west, the sacred and imperishable proclamation of eternal salvation.]]

Luke 24:1-12 But on the first day of the week, at early dawn, they came to the tomb, taking the spices that they had prepared. They found the stone rolled away from the tomb, but when they went in, they did not find the body. While they were perplexed about this, suddenly two men in dazzling clothes stood beside them. The women were terrified and bowed their faces to the ground, but the men said to them, "Why do you look for the living among the dead? He is not here, but has risen. Remember how he told you, while he was still in Galilee, that the Son of Man must be handed over to sinners, and be crucified, and on the third day rise again." Then they remembered his words, and returning from the tomb, they told all this to the eleven and to all the rest. Now it was Mary Magdalene, Joanna, Mary the mother of James, and the other women with them who told this to the apostles. But these words seemed to them an idle tale, and they did not believe them. But Peter got up and ran to the tomb; stooping and looking in, he saw the linen cloths by themselves; then he went home, amazed at what had happened.

John 20:1-10 Early on the first day of the week, while it was still dark, Mary Magdalene came to the tomb and saw that the stone had been removed from the tomb. So she ran and went to Simon Peter and the other disciple, the one whom Jesus loved, and said to them, "They have taken the Lord out of the tomb, and we do not know where they have laid him." Then Peter and the other disciple set out and went toward the tomb. The two were running together, but the other disciple outran Peter and reached the tomb first. He bent down to look in and saw the linen wrappings lying there, but he did not go in. Then Simon Peter came, following him, and went into the tomb. He saw the linen wrappings lying there, and the cloth that had been on Jesus' head, not lying with the linen wrappings but rolled up in a place by itself. Then the other disciple, who reached the tomb first, also went in, and he saw and believed; for as yet they did not understand the scripture, that he must rise from the dead. Then the disciples returned to their homes.

Matthew 28:9-10 Suddenly Jesus met them and said, "Greetings!" And they came to him, took hold of his feet, and worshiped him. Then Jesus said to them, "Do not be afraid; go and tell my brothers to go to Galilee; there they will see me."

Mark 16:9-11 THE LONGER ENDING OF MARK [[Now after he rose early on the first day of the week, he appeared first to Mary Magdalene, from whom he had cast out seven demons. She went out and told those who had been with him, while they were mourning and weeping. But when they heard that he was alive and had been seen by her, they would not believe it.

John 20:11-18 But Mary stood weeping outside the tomb. As she wept, she bent over to look into the tomb; and she saw two angels in white, sitting where the body of Jesus had been lying, one at the head and the other at the feet. They said to her, "Woman, why are you weeping?" She said to them, "They have taken away my Lord, and I do not know where they have laid him." When she had said this, she turned around and saw Jesus standing there, but she did not know that it was Jesus. Jesus said to her, "Woman, why are you weeping? Whom are you looking for?" Supposing him to be the gardener, she said to him, "Sir, if you have carried him away, tell me where you have laid him, and I will take him away." Jesus said to her, "Mary!" She turned and said to him in Hebrew, "Rabbouni!" (which means Teacher). Jesus said to her, "Do not hold on to me, because I have not yet ascended to the Father. But go to my brothers and say to them, 'I am ascending to my Father and your Father, to my God and your God.' " Mary Magdalene went and announced to the disciples, "I have seen the Lord"; and she told them that he had said these things to her.

Why didn't the disciples go with the women to the tomb at the first opportunity?

If you have ever seen beings like the ones described as the angels who announced the resurrection of Jesus, will you describe them and what happened?

Why are there several different accounts of the first appearance of Jesus after his resurrection?

a. From all the facts, each Gospel writer selected the details that made his point.

b. Each Gospel writer had a different source of information.

c. Most people knew of Mary Magdalene so her part of the story remained in tack and the less known women who were there were not mentioned as often in recounting the story.

d. The women retold the story differently, depending on who was interested in what kind and how many details.

e. Other?

Which Gospel's account of the resurrection of Jesus do you like the best and why?

Who have you told about the risen Christ and what was their reaction?

What have been the most meaningful parts of this study?

Jerusalem Area in the Time of Jesus

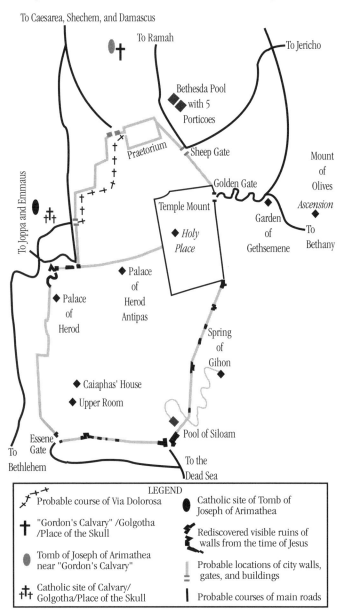

To Caesarea, Shechem, and Damascus

To Ramah

To Jericho

Bethesda Pool
with 5
Porticoes

Praetorium

Sheep Gate

Mount
of
Olives

Golden Gate

To Joppa and Emmaus

Temple Mount

Ascension

Garden
of
Gethsemene

To
Bethany

*Holy
Place*

Palace
of
Herod
Antipas

Palace
of
Herod

Spring
of
Gihon

Caiaphas' House

Upper Room

Pool of Siloam

Essene
Gate

To
Bethlehem

To the
Dead Sea

LEGEND

Probable course of Via Dolorosa

Catholic site of Tomb of
Joseph of Arimathea

"Gordon's Calvary" /Golgotha
/Place of the Skull

Rediscovered visible ruins of
walls from the time of Jesus

Tomb of Joseph of Arimathea
near "Gordon's Calvary"

Probable locations of city walls,
gates, and buildings

Catholic site of Calvary/
Golgotha/Place of the Skull

Probable courses of main roads

Background of Calvary

The word Calvary comes from the Latin word *calvaria. Calvaria*, is a translation of the Greek word *kranion. Kranion* may be compared to our word "cranium". The Greek word *kranion* is translated from the Aramaic word *golgotha.* All three words, the Latin Calvary, the Greek Golgotha, and Aramaic Skull have the same meaning, "skull".

All four Gospels tell the story of the crucifixion of Jesus, referring to the place we call Calvary. However, the word "Calvary" is only used once in the (old and new) King James Versions of the Bible, in Luke 23:33, using Golgotha in the other Gospels. The New Revised Standard Version of the Bible exclusively uses the word *Golgotha*, saying in Matthew 27:33, "...they came to a place called Golgotha (which means Place of a Skull)"; in Mark 15:22, saying, "...they brought Jesus to the place called Golgotha (which means the place of a skull)"; in Luke 23:33, "...they came to the place that is called The Skull"; and in John 19:17, "...he went out to what is called The Place of the Skull, which in Hebrew is called Golgotha."

Explanations for the use of the description of "skull" as the location of the crucifixion of Jesus vary. One explanation is that there were many skulls left unclaimed and accumulating where crucifixions took place. Another explanation is that the hill upon which the crucifixions took place actually looked like a skull.

The scriptures are consistent, saying that Jesus was taken outside of the city to be crucified. A road was in close enough proximity to see or read who was being crucified because there are mentioned passersby who derided Jesus for saying he would destroy the temple and build it in three days. However, the exact location of the crucifixion has never been agreed upon by either scholars or archeologists. Instead, two distinct locations are venerated as the location of the crucifixion. In addition, each of the two locations of the "Place of the Skull" has its own tomb believed to have been given for the burial of Jesus by a rich member of the Sanhedrin, Joseph of Arimathea.

Traditionally, the place first to be thought the location of the crucifixion is the Catholic site called the Church of the Holy Sepulchre. It was first identified in the fourth century by the mother of Emperor Constantine the Great, Queen Helena. After her revelation in a vision the pagan temple that was standing on the site was destroyed and the first of several successive shrines was built on that spot.

It was not until 1842 that the second possible location of the crucifixion of Jesus was introduced. Otto Thenius discovered the site outside the Damascus Gate, but the fame of the rocky hill was gained only after Charles Gordon declared it so in writing about 1885. Only then did the nearby garden tomb, which was discovered in 1849, attract much attention.

Over time, the local geography has been so radically altered that it is impossible to verify the actual site of the crucifixion. Good cases have been made for the authenticity of both the Catholic site and Gordon's Calvary. Mike Mitchell, writing for the *Holman Bible Dictionary,* leans on the side of the Catholic site. Mitchell asserts that, first, the outer wall of Jerusalem was much closer to the center of the city at the time of the crucifixion. Second, the tomb venerated at the Catholic site is more like those of the traditional Jewish tombs, being a small carved out niche in a wall rather than the Byzantine trough-type slab in the garden near the site of Gordon's Calvary.

Crucifixion

Crucifixion was adopted by the Romans for execution, but was first used in Persia and Carthage. Generally, Roman citizens were not crucified. Crucifixion was used only for the punishment of political criminals, slaves, foreigners, and thieves.

It has been said that the cruelest punishment of all times is crucifixion. The entire process is a torturous ordeal for the condemned. Physical tortures, mental abuse, and emotional taunts were incorporated into this ritual death sentence. Officials, onlookers, and passersby were all part of the torment projected at the man who hung on the cross.

Recently, archeologists have made discoveries that shed light on more of the particulars of crucifixion. Where the cross is concerned, around the time of the crucifixion of Jesus, an upright stake was probably in place on Golgotha. To the permanent stake (gibbet) was added the crossbeam which the convicted man carried to his execution. When the crossbeam was slipped into a groove on top of the stake, a "T" shape was formed. With the man's shoulders and arms spread wide across the crossbeam and his head rising above, the form of a cross upon a hilltop was observed for miles as a cruel warning to others.

Arms were tied or nailed to the cross. Skeletal remains of a young man crucified in the first century show that his wrists were punctured with something like large Roman carpenter's nails made of iron. The same type of spike was used to cause a puncture that went through both heel bones or ankles as one wound.

Because the body weight of the victim was supported only by straddling a large peg, his contorted frame could only be held in a position to breathe for a limited amount of time. As the dead weight of his body grew heavier and he was less able to raise himself to a breathing position, the oxygen deprived blood slowly built up carbon dioxide which created great demands on his heart. Without sufficient oxygen his muscles contracted, causing cramps and wrenching spasms.

The victim of crucifixion was alive for only as long as he could cope with or ward off his torments. He was confined prey, subject to swarms of irritating buzzing and biting insects, as well as eager predators. His naked body was further assaulted by the weather's scorching heat, bitter cold, driving drains, or cutting winds. From within the victim suffered both hunger pangs and parching thirst.

It could take two to three days for the condemned to die. For the sake of convenience, to expedite the process for the officials or to remove the dead before the Jewish Holy days, the legs of the condemned would be broken. Then he could die quickly by either of two ways. By breaking his legs, he could not raise himself up to open his diaphragm and gasp another breath, and without air he would die of suffocation or asphyxiation. Or, with the crushing pressure of his hanging weight on his chest he would suffer heart failure. Loss of blood was not the primary cause of death.

But the unclaimed crucified carcase could also remain on its cross until picked clean or until the gibbet was needed for another crucifixion. Nearly 100 years before the crucifixion of Jesus, the Via Appia in Rome was lined with crosses. About 6,000 slaves hung on them. They were executed for following Spartacus, a slave-gladiator. Church tradition says that Peter was crucified upside-down by his own request to signify that he felt unworthy to die in the same manner as Jesus had.

Resurrection

In the New Revised Standard Version of the Bible "eternal life" is mentioned in 43 verses in the New Testament, according to macBible 3.0. Forty-two verses mention "resurrection". The author of Hebrews, in calling the first century believers to move on to maturity, includes the resurrection of the dead as one of the basic foundations of the faith (Hebrews 5:14-6:2). However, resurrection has been a controversial doctrine since its inception.

Briefly, in its purest form, resurrection is the doctrine of a belief in a unified body, soul and spirit living after death. 1Thessalonians 5:23 is a prayer that God sanctify the believer entirely—spirit and soul and body—to be kept "sound and blameless" until Jesus comes again to reunite all believers at the end of the world. Without all three, body, soul, and spirit, it is believed that there can be no true life. Nations and religions other than the Hebrews believed in resurrection, but not always for the triune being. For example, in the first century the Greeks immortal and independent soul was without body or spirit.

However, the concept of resurrection was not always a Hebrew doctrine. It was not until after the Babylonian exile that the concept of resurrection became a doctrine of the Hebrews. Resurrection was widely accepted by the time of Jesus. However, the Sadducees were one notable exception. Along with no angels and no spirit, they rejected the concept because it was not clearly stated in the Pentateuch (Acts 23:8). Romans 6:5 tells us that if we are united with Jesus in a death like his—spiritually speaking—then we will be united with Jesus in a resurrection like his—body, soul, and spirit.

Of the Body

The Old Testament speaks of an awakening of individuals who were sleeping in the dust of the earth (Daniel 12:2). Jesus predicted that the graves would open and the dead would hear the voice of the Lord and come out. The good would enter into resurrection life and the evil to eternal condemnation (John 5:28-29). The fulfillment of the prediction of Jesus came about when the tombs were opened when the earth quaked and the rocks split and the Temple veil was torn from top to bottom when Jesus died. Afterward, many *bodies* of the "saints who had fallen asleep" were raised from the dead and went into Jerusalem. The Bible says that many people saw the saints in the city (Matthew 27:52-53).

In the New Testament, the Apostle Paul insists that our "perishable body" will have to "put on imperishability" as our mortal body will have to don immortality (1Corinthians 15:53). The writer of Acts 2:31 quotes King David and his prophesy regarding the resurrection of the Messiah. Then the fulfillment is noted because Jesus did not stay in Hades, nor did he experience any corruption or decay of his body. To the contrary, Jesus reappeared after death with a physical body that ate, drank, and bore the physical scars of his life on earth, but transcended earthly bounds to move freely and appear and disappear at will (Luke 24:36-43; John 20:24-28).

Hebrews 11:35a we are reminded of the faithful women and men who witnessed resurrection. Unnamed in Hebrews, but clearly identified in the Gospels are Martha, the widow of Nain, and Jairus. One was a beloved friend who questioned Jesus, one was a weeping stranger who did not ask Jesus, and one was a religious leader seeking Jesus, but each experienced the resurrection of their dead relative—body, soul, and spirit.

Of the Soul

In Matthew 10:28 we are warned that we should not fear the forces able to kill the body and not kill the soul. However, we should fear who or whatever can utterly destroy the soul and the body in hell throughout eternity. The soul of the sinner who strays from God's ways will die. But while on this earth the straying sinner's soul can be saved and sins forgiven when we bring back the sinner to the ways of God (James 5:20). God's ideal is that the soul be preserved not just until the resurrection and judgements, but throughout eternity (1Thesalonians 5:23). The resurrection of the soul can be witnessed in the recounts of Jesus and his interactions after his resurrection. His mind, will, and emotions were all functional in his resurrected body, along with his resurrected spirit.

Of the Spirit

In resurrection there is a higher realm of the spirit for us. In the resurrection we will be like the angels in heaven (Luke 20:36; Matthew 22:30; Mark 12:25). One example of the difference between our state now and our spirit's resurrection, is like the angels, our concerns will no longer be for earthly things, but instead for spiritual, Godly things—As are the angels in Heaven, now! Luke 14:14 promises that deeds done by the righteous will receive a reward at "the resurrection of the righteous." Righteousness is a state of our spirit. Therefore, to be spiritually judged and rewarded, our spirits must be resurrected.

Reflection

Mary Magdalene was chosen by Jesus to be the first to see the resurrection. She was chosen by Jesus to be the first to hear of his resurrection by Jesus himself. It was Mary Magdalene whom Jesus chose to be the first to proclaim the Good News of the Gospel: The Resurrection!

It was not a coincidence that she was near the tomb weeping when Jesus found her. She had been near him while he traveled in his ministry. She had remained near the cross during his crucifixion. She had sat near the tomb when he was laid to rest. And she had remained near his heart through it all.

Jesus knew Mary's heart toward him. Jesus knew Mary's dedication to him. Jesus knew Mary's dependability for him. Jesus knew Mary. But more importantly, Mary knew Jesus.

She had been set free by Jesus. Because of him seven demons had gone out of her. With that in mind, Gien Karssen writes in her Book Two of *Her Name is Woman:*

> Mary Magdalene wanted to stay close to Jesus for many reasons. First, she knew by experience that she could not afford to minimize the power of Satan. Unless she stayed close to the Lord—who was superior to the devil—she alone would have no defense against Satan's attacks. She had to prevent the evil one from possessing her again. If that should happen, her end would be worse than before (Luke 11:24-26).

But Mary Magdalene did not stay close to Jesus for selfish reasons or just to protect herself from further misfortune. Mary had followed Jesus, provided for him, and served him throughout his ministry—even into death. Virginia Stem Owens reminds us that others wanted to follow Jesus, such as the Gerasene demoniac, but Jesus sent him and others away. Yet, Mary Magdalene became a constant follower and provider for Jesus, without any hint that he ever tried to send her away. She is among the devoted women who not only follow Jesus, but provide for him along with the twelve male disciples. In *Daughters of Eve*, Owens writes, "More likely, she is added to the entourage because she possesses some particular skill or aptitude . . . . all these women are mentioned because they have a particular contribution to make."

Mary Magdalene made many contributions to Jesus and his ministry. She was one of Jesus' most trusted disciples. She was the leader of the other women.

When they travelled with him in his ministry, when they followed him from Galilee, when they walked with him on the Via Dolorosa, when they stood by him at Calvary, when they prepared burial spices for him the eve before the sabbath, when they came at early dawn to his tomb on the first day of the week, when they saw and heard the angels proclaim his resurrection, when they saw and heard the risen Lord, when they went to the disciples to proclaim his resurrection—always, Mary Magdalene was their leader.

So much was entrusted to her and the other women who followed, served, and provided for Jesus out of their own means. Carla Ricci, author of *Mary Magdalene and Many Others: Women who followed Jesus,* makes a convincing argument for Mary Magdalene, Joanna, Susanna, Salome, and Mary the mother of James to be women in part of a group, along with other unnamed women, who comprised a comparable group of female apostles just as do the twelve male apostles of Jesus. The contrasts between Mary Magdalene and Peter on the adjoining page are a result of my pondering Carla Ricci's thought below. She writes that:

> If from what we have seen so far, it is possible to see an analogy between the group of the twelve and the group of women, and between the inner group of three apostles and the inner group of three women, then the conclusion to be drawn is that the figure of Mary Magdalene should be seen in equal terms with that of Peter, who receives so much more attention in the texts.

According to the second century *Gospel of Mary* in the Egyptian Gnostic writings, Mary Magdalene was the closest, most loved spiritual companion of Jesus. She was the only one who really understood spiritual matters and became the teacher and interpreter of the mysteries of faith for the male disciples. At times, the writings break out into overt anger, jealousy, and rejection through the dialogue which pinpoints some male resentment toward this most notable female protagonist. Specifically, on one occasion, the Lord's Apostle Levi rebukes Peter for always being angry and mistreating and rejecting Mary Magdalene—even though Peter knows full well that Jesus loved Mary Magdalene most of all and entrusted her with his message.

In the third century writing of Pistis-Sophia, Mary tells Jesus that she is afraid of Peter because he threatens her and hates women. If the dialogue is accurate, Mary's perception may have been more farsighted than

Contrasts in Leader Experiences: Peter and Mary Magdalene

Peter was given a new name after meeting Jesus (Mark 3:16; Luke 6:14; John 1:42).

Mary kept the same name after meeting Jesus.

Peter saw the transfiguration of Jesus (Matt. 17:1-4; Mark 9:2-6; Luke 9:28-36).

Mary saw the crucifixion of Jesus (Matt. 27:56; Mark 15:40; John 19:25).

Peter heard God's voice from Heaven proclaim his Son, Jesus (Matthew 17:5; Mark 9:7; Luke 9:35).

Mary heard the voice of Jesus proclaim that his father God had forsaken him (Matt. 27:46; Mark 15:34).

Peter asked Jesus if he must forgive seven times (Matt. 18:21).

Mary was delivered of seven demons by Jesus (Luke 8:2)

Peter told Jesus that he had left everything to follow him (Matt. 19:27; Mark 10:28; Luke 18:28).

Mary provided for Jesus as she followed him (Luke 8:1-3)

Peter fell asleep in the Garden after Jesus asked him to remain watching and praying with him (Matt. 26:37-46; Mark 14:33-42).

Mary stood in the Garden watching and weeping for Jesus without being asked to (John 20:11-17; Mark 16:9).

Peter denied Jesus to strangers (Matt. 26:58-75; Mark 14:54-72; Luke 22:54-62; John 18:15-27).

Mary proclaimed Jesus risen to the disciples (Luke 24:10; John 20:18).

Peter fled from the cross (Matt. 26:56; Mark 14:27-29).

Mary remained near the cross (Matt. 27:56; Mark 15:40; John 19:25).

Peter was sent a message from Jesus (Mark 16:7).

Mary was given a message by Jesus (Luke 24:10; John 20:18).

Peter left the empty tomb without understanding (John 20:6-10).

Mary remained at the empty tomb, the last place she saw Jesus, and had an encounter with him (John 20:11-17; Mark 16:9).

to see just Peter in that role. Perhaps Mary Magdalene was the first woman devoted to Jesus and his ministry to endure the misunderstanding, misrepresentation, and mistreatment of others who were not as close to the Lord or entrusted with as much.

Over the years Mary has been discredited and demoted to a demon possessed prostitute. She is absent from all New Testament Church events recorded in the Bible. As an example, for whatever reason, the Apostle Paul omitted her from the list of those who had seen Jesus after his resurrection and wrote that Jesus first appeared to Peter.

Resentment or envy may be motivators to discredit Mary Magdalene and demote her from her leadership role in the ministry of Jesus, both before and after his resurrection. Joyce Hollyday, author of *Clothed with the Sun: Biblical Women, Social Justice & Us,* writes that "She got too close to Jesus for comfort, from the perspective of all those men who wanted the inner circle to include only Peter and James and John." Hollyday's idea has been developed by a number of religious scholars who have written books on this slant regarding the negative attitudes toward Mary Magdalene and other Bible women, as well as our foremothers and women today.

Carla Ricci gets right at the idea of negative attitudes when she points out that all manner of pictures have been composed, but "what has been written and portrayed of Mary Magdalene is nothing other than a kind of photographic negative, from which the real image of the author can be developed." Many other reputable voices defend Mary Magdalene and her place of value in the pre- and post-resurrection ministry of Jesus.

For voices to the contrary, which are not included

in this Reflection, the reader may consult a bookstore or library—church or public—for a plethora of books written to condemn or extol the Mary Magdalene who they inaccurately portray as the woman caught in adultery and brought before Jesus by the scribes and Pharisees to trap him with a question about the law of Moses; and again as the prostitute sinner who: wept, washed, and anointed the feet of Jesus at the house of Simon the Pharisee early in the ministry of Jesus; and in another incarnation she appears as the sinful, selfish, rebellious sister of Martha and Lazarus.

But never do such books, chapters, or comments commend the participation of Mary Magdalene in Jesus' ministry or her leadership among the women and other disciples in the early church. When Mary Magdalene is portrayed in the third century tradition, her sole purpose is for men and especially women to observe the sinful who was down and through submission was elevated to the status of a messenger without respect, who's message was not believed.

However, the more accurate picture of Mary Magdalene is of a woman who was set free from her demons, by Jesus, so that she could be fully woman, fully friend, fully a follower, and fully a leader providing for Jesus and those with him. This Mary Magdalene is a role-model of active service in full participation, first for the development of the ministry of Jesus and later the Christian church community of the first century.

In another attempt to defend Mary Magdalene with the printed Word of God, this chapter contains all known scripture references to Mary Magdalene. The scriptures have been included so that the reader will be able to base the concept of Mary Magdalene on what the Bible says about her, rather than what oral or written commentators have used for effect or worse yet, out of ignorance. Let us look more closely, once again, at the scriptures associated with Mary Magdalene.

The reader will notice that in the scriptures nowhere is Mary Magdalene identified as a prostitute or even a sinner. Her greatest detraction—if it is a detraction at all—is that Jesus cast seven demons out of her. In a variety of persons, Jesus cast out many demons associated with sickness, disease, malfunction, and insanity. No one knows what were the demons of Mary Magdalene. Joyce Hollyday, hypothesizes that "...[M]aybe herdemons' were the resentment, anger, and envy that take root in a gifted and charismatic woman when a society denies her an opportunity to give and lead."

Finally, whoever or whatever Mary Magdalene has or has not been portrayed as, her biblical record testifies of her dedication and steadfastness to Jesus. We know that it was this woman who followed him from Galilee, providing for and ministering to him. We know that Mary Magdalene was honored by being named among the relatives of Jesus near the cross. She is also mentioned as lingering with his corpse until he was out of sight in the sealed tomb. She was named first in the encounters with angels and Jesus, and in carrying the first message of the resurrection. All these facts are clear in the scriptures.

But it takes more than intellect to understand the intent and meaning of the scriptures—it takes the guidance and inspiration of the Holy Spirit. Let us all approach the scriptures in openness, to receive the level of revelation we are able. Then let us seek the greater truths of the mysteries of God contained in the Holy Scriptures.

Mary Magdalene

Matthew 27:56-61; 28:1-11; Mark 15:40-47; 16:10;
Luke 8:1-3; 24:1-12; John 19:25; 20:1-2, 11-18

Mary Magdalene may be the woman most often confused for someone else! People have mistaken her for the sister of Martha and Lazarus, the sinner woman who was first to anoint Jesus, and a prostitute. Mary Magdalene was none of these. She was, however, a devout follower, supporter, and friend of Jesus. She traveled with him as he taught and healed; she stayed with him as he hung on the cross; she wept for him at his empty tomb. A reward for her steadfastness was to be the first person to see Jesus in his glorified, resurrected body—before he ascended to his Father in Heaven. Later, Jesus returned and showed himself to the disciples and scolded them for not believing Mary Magdalene who had carried Jesus' message to them.

Focus Virtue: Steadfastness

Therefore, my beloved, be steadfast, immovable,
always excelling in the work of the Lord,
because you know that in the Lord
your labor is not in vain.

1Corinthians 15:58

Jesus cast seven demons (physical? mental? spiritual?) out of this woman from Magdala, a bustling port on the Sea of Galilee. Is that what it takes for a person to be steadfast, immovable, always serving the Lord? If so, we need to look into our own lives and hearts and number the demons that Jesus has cast out for us—or even prevented from entering in the first place. When we clearly see what the Lord has done for us, then we will behave so that our steadfastness in all circumstances will be seen and hailed as has been the steadfastness of Mary Magdalene.

I will demonstrate my steadfastness by remaining
faithful and purposeful through tests and obstacles,
no matter how bad or good the circumstances.

Virtues Reflection:
Mary Magdalene

Mary Magdalene is one of the women in the Gospels who is able to teach us a variety of things when we look at her from the perspective of a role model of Christian virtues. Mary demonstrated virtues that are to be admired and emulated, such as generosity, faithfulness, and loyalty. Also, she can teach us about our need to exercise our virtues, purposefully, in the face of defeat. In addition, Mary demonstrated that the need for further development of our virtues, as well as their full use is important because even Mary's virtues of awareness and understanding were not being utilized enough on that resurrection morning when she questioned the gardener about the location of the body of Jesus.

Today, when you read about, think on, and discuss the stories that include Mary Magdalene, identify the developed virtues you see in her. *(You may want to review the Focus Virtues list in Chapter One.)*

1. Which developed virtue of Mary Magdalene do you most appreciate, today?

2. How has this virtue been part of your life in the past or in the present?

3. How do you see this virtue or the need for it in your life, now?

4. What can you do to further develop this virtue in your life?

5. What has been the most valuable part of this study?

Action Scripture

Matthew 28:17-20 *When they saw him, they worshiped him; but some doubted. And Jesus came and said to them, "All authority in heaven and on earth has been given to me. Go therefore and make disciples of all nations, baptizing them in the name of the Father and of the Son and of the Holy Spirit, and teaching them to obey everything that I have commanded you. And remember, I am with you always, to the end of the age."*

Grateful Prayer

Redeemer God, You have given us the greatest gift of all, redemption through Your Son Jesus. Our hearts rejoice and our lips praise You. We give glory to You for Your gift of life eternal in Your presence. We thank you that we can come into Your presence, now. As we rest in Your presence, lay Your healing hand upon us. Fill us with strength to endure and overcome every obstacle that prevents us from living the abundant life in Christ Jesus. Even in our doubt, grant us grace to believe and go forth to do Your will. Show us how we can go in the authority of Jesus' name and make disciples. Show us how to fulfill our part in teaching them to obey everything that Jesus commanded—that we love God with all our heart, with all our soul, with all our mind, and with all our strength, and to love others as much as we love ourselves. Bless those with an open heart so that they, just as Mary Magdalene did, may see Jesus and hear him speak their name in comfort and with guidance. We ask all these things in the name of Jesus Christ our Lord, so that You, Eternal God, may be glorified, AMEN.

Selected References & Readings

macBible 3.0 (1993). Grand Rapids, MI: Zondervan.

Microsoft Encarta Encyclopedia. 1996 Edition. U.S.A.: Microsoft Corp.

Bellis, Alice Ogden (1994). *Helpmates, Harlots, and Heroes: Women's Stories in the Hebrew Bible.* Louisville, KY: Westminister John Knox.

Bouquet, A.C. (1954). *Everyday Life in New Testament Times.* New York Charles Scribner's Sons.

Brestin, Dee (1996). *We Are Sisters.* Wheaton, IL: Victor.

Bristow, John Temple (1988). *What Paul Really Said About Women: An Apostle's Liberating Views on Equality in Marriage, Leadership, and Love.* San Francisco: HarperCollins.

Buchmann, Christina, and Spiegel, Celina (Eds.) (1995). *Out of the Garden: Women Writers on the Bible.* New York: Fawcett Columbine.

Bultmann, Rudolf Karl (1971). *The Gospel of John.* Philadelphia: Westminister.

Butler, Trent C. (Ed. et al.) (1991). *Holman Bible Dictionary.* Nashville: Holman.

Carpenter, Christine M. (1995). *All the Women in the Bible: Sisters and Sisterhood.* Portland, OR: CMC Press.

Chadwick, John W., et al. (1902). *Women of the Bible*. New York: Harper.

Deen, Edith (1955). *All of the Women of the Bible*. New York: Harper & Row.

Alexander, David, Alexander, Pat (Eds.) (1973). *Eerdmans' Handbook to the Bible*. Grand Rapids, MI: Wm. B. Eerdmans.

Grosvenor, Melville Bell, & Vosburgh, Frederick G. (Eds.) (1967). *Everyday Life in Bible Times*. Washington, D.C.: National Geographic Society.

Harrison, Eveleen (1936). *Little-Known Women of the Bible*. New York: Round Table.

Hollyday, Joyce (1994). *Clothed with the Sun: Biblical Women, Social Justice, and Us*. Louisville, KY: Westminister John Knox.

Josephus, Flavius (1987). *The Works of Josephus*, Trans., William Whiston. Peabody, MA: Hendrickson.

Karssen, Gien (1975). *Her Name Is Woman*. Colorado Springs, CO: NavPress.

Karssen, Gien (1977). *Her Name Is Woman: Book 2*. Colorado Springs, CO: NavPress.

Lockyer, Herbert (1993). *All the Women of the Bible: The Life and Times of All the Women of the Bible*. Grand Rapids, MI: Zondervan.

McKay, John P., Hill, Bennett D., & Buckler, John (1987). *History of Western Society*. Boston, MA: Houghton Mifflin.

Mead, Frank S. (1934). *Who's Who in the Bible: 250 Bible Biographies.* New York: Harper & Row.

Miller, Madeleine S., & Miller, J. Lane (1955). *Encyclopedia of Bible Life.* New York: Harper.

Miller, Madeleine S., & Miller, J. Lane (1959). *Harper's Bible Dictionary.* New York: Harper.

Moltmann-Wendel, Elisabeth (1982). *The Women Around Jesus.* New York: Crossroad.

Mosley, Jean Bell (1960). *Know Your Bible Program: Famous Women of the New Testament.* Garden City, NY: Nelson Doubleday.

Nelson, Hazel McCurdy (1958). *Bible Women Come Alive.* New York: Abingdon.

Newsom, Carol A., Ringe, Sharon H. (Eds) (1992). *The Women's Bible Commentary.* Louisville, KY: Westminister/John Knox.

Nunnally-Cox, Janice (1981). *Fore-Mothers: Women of the Bible.* New York: Sebury.

Owens, Virginia Stem (1995). *Daughters of Eve: Women of the Bible Speak to Women of Today.* Colorado Springs, CO: NavPress.

Phipps, William E. (1992). *Assertive Biblical Women.* Westport, CT: Greenwood.

Pope, Jr., John A. (Ed. et al.) (1991). *ABC's of the Bible.* New York: Reader's Digest.

Price, Eugenia (1969). *The Unique World of Women.* Grand Rapids, MI: Zondervan.

Ricci, Carla (1994). *Mary Magdalene and Many Others: Women who followed Jesus,* Trans., Paul Burns. Minneapolis: Fortress.

Sellier, Charles E., & Russell, Brian (1994). *Ancient Secrets of the Bible.* New York: Dell.

Sessions, Will (1958). *Greater Men and Women of the Bible.* St. Louis, MO: Bethany.

Stanton, Elizabeth Cady (1974, reprint). *The Woman's Bible.* Seattle, WA: Coalition Task Force on Women and Religion.

Tillich, Paul (1955). *The New Being.* New York: Scribner.

Wold, Margaret (1987). *Women of Faith and Spirit.* Minneapolis, MN: Augsburg.

Wright, G. Ernest (Ed. et al.) (1974). *Great People of the Bible and How They Lived.* New York: Reader's Digest.

Index

251

The Instant Bible Study!

Everything you need to start, run, grow, and enjoy an
All the Women in the Bible study group—
just select the topic in the series (listed below) and add the people!

Sisters & Sisterhood
Mothers & Daughters
Wives, Widows & Concubines
Influential Bible Women
Bible Women of Great Faith
All The Women Around Jesus

Program Contents

Promotional Materials for Reproduction

- Newsletter Articles: Teasers, Announcements, and Reminders
- Fliers & Posters: For Churches, Businesses, and Community
- Personal Letters, Announcements, Invitations, and Reminders
- Promotional Skits to Interest and Motivate Attendance
- Media Releases and Supplemental Information for Promotion
- "Brainstorm" Sheets with Separate Answer Sheets

Facilitator Helps

- Facilitator Tips, Training Bulletins, and Group Leader Skills
- Marketing/Promotion Plan, Strategies, and Schedules
- Contact Suggestions, Scripts, and Follow-up Options
- Agendas Listed by Formats: 1 Hour, 1 $\frac{1}{2}$ Hours, or 2 Hours
- Supply and Task Lists: Needed, Have, and Do
- Facilitator's Guide: Activities, Materials, and What to Do
  - Detailed Activities and Exercises For:
    - Gathering before the meeting
    - Starting the meeting
    - Getting acquainted
    - "Brainstorming"
    - Forming small groups
    - Small group leadership selection
    - Group sharing
    - Discussion Questions
    - Closing sharing
    - Prayers and parting rituals

For more information write CMC Press, P.O. Box 8716, Portland, Oregon 97207

Sisters & Sisterhood Materials

Why Read or Play Sisters & Sisterhood?

- Do you want to know the women in the Bible as well as you know the men in the Bible? If you read this book you will begin to better know the Bible women.

- Do you want to see and experience the women in the Bible as real people to whom you can relate in your own life situations? If you read this book you will begin to better know the ways of success and failure through the Bible women.

- Do you want to expand your understanding of yourself and all women? If you read this book you will begin to better know who you are by knowing more of your heritage, roots, and traditions found in the women in the Bible.

- Do you want to learn how to draw out and use the virtues within yourself and others? If you read this book you will begin to better identify virtues within yourself and others and move toward using them to better your world and that of others.

What will be the benefits of reading or playing Sisters & Sisterhood?

- You will know more of what others believe about the women in the Bible.

- You will know more of what you believe about the women in the Bible.

- You will know more of what you believe about the role of a woman today.

- You will know more of what you can do to have virtuous attitudes and behaviors surround you.

Is it true, what they say about Sisters?

ALL THE WOMEN IN THE BIBI SISTERS & SISTERHOOD
This book for individual or group devc or study is divided into six sections focu on: An overview of all the sisters in Bible, Lot's Daughters, Leah & Rac Zelophehad's Daughters, Martha & M and Bernice & Drusilla; scriptures questions to consider; factual backgro about locale, times, and customs; fa trees and maps; Bible woman summa Focus Virtues; Reflections and tod applications; Action Scriptures; Grateful Prayers.

ALL THE WOMEN IN THE BIBL SISTERS & SISTERHOOD PROGRAM BINDER
Designed to support church growth spiritual development in a group sett this binder contains: Facilitator He Facilitator's Guide, Support Materials, Promotional Materials. From fliers newsletter articles through get-acquai activities and closing exercises, program binder is a helpful resource instant, easy, fun group formation, gro or propagation.

BIBLE WOMAN SURPRISE CAR
Each of 52 5 $\frac{1}{2}$" x 8 $\frac{1}{2}$" card contains name of a Bible woman; script references to her story; a brief summary her life; a Focus Virtue she modelec Focus Virtue scripture; how her Fo Virtue was demonstrated; ways the Fo Virtue can be part of our lives, tod concluding with a positive affirmation us the Focus Virtue. Cards are on seve different colors of card stock. A 53rd c lists all 52 selected Focus Virtues and Fo Virtue Exercises for individuals and grou Great for individual daily devotions and group get-acquainted or devotio activities.

by The Reverend Christine Carpenter

What are the New Games Sisters Play?

SISTERS & SISTERHOOD MONOPOLY TYPE TABLE GAME

The object of the game is to win while maintaining Sisterhood. The winner is the player who has accumulated the most life points when the game ends. Players draw Gift Cards when completing one life cycle—turn around the board—while players produce Progeny, Become Productive, Secure Property, and Acquire Privilege. Other draw cards include: Circumstances of Birth; Chosen Production; Current Status of Holdings; Rights of Status; and Court Card.

SISTERS & SISTERHOOD TRIVIA TYPE CARD GAME

Over 300 questions about all the sisters and sisterhood in the Bible are included in this game that can be played by everyone interested in learning more about the women in the Bible. Designed for beginner, intermediate, and advanced levels. Answers are printed on the reverse side of 4 1/4" x 5 1/2" cardstock printed with questions. Instructions are included for several variations of the original Trivia style game.

SISTERS & SISTERHOOD BINGO TYPE GUESSING GAME

Here is a Sisters & Sisterhood twist to the original style BINGO—plus other variations to adapt to the whim of your group or party guests. Contents include: Instructions; 10 SISTERS BINGO cards for version one; 10 SISTERS BINGO cards for version two; 1 SISTERS BINGO number and letter names and descriptions; 3 SISTERS BINGO card one game variations; 4 BINGO CARD two game variations; 1 each Leader's Master List for card one and card 2; and 1 SISTERS BINGO Clue Sheet.

Order Form: Send a completed copy of this order form with full payment in check or money order in U.S. currency to: CMC Press, P.O. Box 8716, Portland, OR 97207.

Qty.		Price	Amount
	Sisters & Sisterhood Book	16.95	
	Sisters & Sisterhood Program Binder	34.95	
	Bible Woman Surprise Cards	12.95	
	Sisters & Sisterhood MONOPOLY Type Board Game	16.95	
	Sisters & Sisterhood TRIVIA Type Card Game	16.95	
	Sisters & Sisterhood BINGO Type Guessing Game	16.95	
	Focus Virtue (18" x 24", colored) Poster	12.95	
	Focus Virtue Wallet Cards (50 cards and holder)	5.95	
	Focus Virtue Refrigerator Magnet (business card size)	2.00	
	TOTAL AMOUNT $		

*Request a FREE brochure describing audio cassettes of KSET News or of specific Bible women cameo presentations—hear her tell her story!

[For Video Tapes of Bible Women or quantity discounts on materials, please call 503/228-6003 or 1-800/914-7988]

Please PRINT clearly; this will be your shipping label.

Name _____

Street_____

City/State/ZIP_____